DANIELLE MASSI, LMFT

shadow work

Face Hidden Fears, Heal Trauma, Awaken Your Dream Life

STERLING ETHOS
New York

STERLING ETHOS
New York

ISBN 978-1-4549-4647-2 (hardcover)
ISBN 978-1-4549-4648-9 (e-book)

For information about custom editions, special sales,
and premium purchases, please contact
specialsales@unionsquareandco.com.

Printed in the United States of America

2 4 6 8 10 9 7 5 3 1

unionsquareandco.com

Interior design: Jordan Wannemacher
Cover design: Jordan Wannemacher

Crafter/Creative Market: cover; throughout;
Shutterstock.com: ArcTina: 21;
lavendertime: 98; Monory: 19

*This book is dedicated to my late
mentor, Allison Kelsey.
Thank you for introducing me
to the beauty of shadow work,
and for always seeing the magic in me.*

Contents

Foreword

I was thrilled when my beloved teacher, Danielle Massi, invited me to write some opening words for her book about shadow work. I have been a clinical psychologist in private practice for twenty years, and nothing has impacted me more deeply than working with her to connect to my shadow. (Coincidentally, Danielle and I had offices in the same downtown Philadelphia building for years prior to the COVID-19 pandemic but had never met.) In my decade of graduate work, and in my time working in hospitals, college counseling centers, and residential treatment centers, I have studied everything from neuroscience to cognitive-behavioral theory to positive psychology to psychoanalysis. In addition, I've been in therapy off and on since my early twenties, including an analysis, multiple times a week, for twelve years. I've also taken antidepressants during a family health crisis and the early child-rearing years. I've meditated, done yoga, had acupressure/acupuncture/energy healing, pursued years of psychic training and intuition building, studied my astrology and human design charts, done EFT/tapping and neuro-emotional technique, and even trained as a Reiki master. I have been tireless in my pursuit of healing, and each step has brought me more information, more personal insight, and definitely more relief.

However, while psychoanalysis and these other healing modalities worked with the edges of my pain, as well as the behaviors I had developed to cope with my pain, it was my introduction to shadow work that allowed me to get to the core of my issues. One of the most difficult points of my healing has been a disturbing relationship with my mother. While there are plenty of adult interactions that I remember, much of the psychological, spiritual, and emotional abuse happened at such a young age that it's effectively suppressed and tucked away. In fact, I did not consciously detect any difficulties in this relationship until I moved across the country at age twenty-four. At that point, it slowly started to dawn on me each time I visited home, that she wasn't in fact my best friend, and that she was struggling with serious mental illness. I spent many years in my twenties and thirties in therapy, trying to untangle this relationship, reading our email exchanges to my therapist to help me dissect them and strategize ways to protect myself more effectively. (In fairness to my younger self, my teen years had been about my father coming out of the closet, and the impact that had on him, his job, and our family, as we were entrenched in an evangelical religion in the buckle of the Bible belt.)

Each time I moved forward in my life—getting married, moving away to graduate school, completing my PhD, getting married again, having babies—my mother decompensated and became strangely aggressive. However, when I got divorced during graduate school, she became momentarily sane and helpful, somehow visiting Philadelphia to help me pack my young husband's things, as he had already taken what he could and had driven back to the Midwest. At the same time, she took the opportunity to remark on my apparent hubris, how at the age of twenty-four, I thought I could marry my college sweetheart *AND* go to graduate school on the East Coast. She reminded me of the sheer greediness of it all . . . that I had wanted *BOTH*.

Through the years, I've had support in setting boundaries with my mother, as many others have witnessed her behavior, borne partly out of her own trauma history. But it's been hard to explain my fear of her—my sense that I was dealing with more than just narcissism or a borderline personality. I have made the heart-wrenching decision not to communicate with her for almost a decade now, except for two visits home when she had a brief psychotic break and could no longer live alone. During one of our sessions, my analyst shared that he'd had a nightmare the week before, in which he woke with a start and sat up in complete terror. At that moment, I came to his mind and he thought, *this is exactly how terrified*

Allison is of her mother. This is what she's been trying to tell me. The closest I had gotten to explaining the spiritual darkness in my childhood was in the screams of the Echthroi, or demonic monsters, in Madeleine L'Engle's books, which I had read ravenously as a very young child. While I didn't fully understand why, those stories of love casting out evil were enlightening and soothing for my young psyche.

For me, many of the answers about this darkness have been found in shadow work with Danielle Massi. Deep in meditation, thus accessing my unconscious, I have been shown exactly what has transpired between my mother and me, during this lifetime and across many lifetimes. During these powerful sessions, I was able to safely observe and reexperience the trauma, changing my body's relationship to it as well as distancing myself from it and healing from its impacts. While there have been layers of trauma and shadow to examine and peel back (I've been doing this work for over a year now), the work on this theme has been the most powerful in terms of my healing. It has begun to have far-reaching impacts such as setting boundaries with less anxiety and guilt, ending or redefining codependent relationships, guarding my energy carefully, and engaging more deeply in seeking pleasure and joy. For me, it's been a game changer.

Danielle Massi is a powerhouse of a teacher, holding space in person, or on the page, in an incredibly grounded yet electrified way. She has the profound ability to take you right to your learning edge, right to where you need to be. A recent photograph depicts her dressed in a long gown, in the middle of the woods at dusk, holding a lantern above her head to guide the way for others. This represents her energy perfectly. Danielle is the quintessential way-shower, a guide into the dark and then back out again, defying her chronological age and holding a wealth of experience that indicates that she's done this work for lifetimes. As the saying goes, "This is not her first rodeo."

Danielle Massi is someone who decided that her cancer diagnosis, treatment, and the depression that followed were her breaking point, her personal rock bottom, and her reason to swim even a little deeper to find out what was there—what was stuck in her body and her psyche, in her unconscious tales about herself. She might not tell you this, but this process took immense grit, courage, persistence, and bravery. She had to believe in herself and her process even before it was completely developed. What Danielle has done for us here is to lay out a map or a template for the journey. There's something in here for everyone—the mystic, the scientist, the poet, and the student. So, dear reader, grab your journal, a candle, and a cup of tea or cacao. Pull up a chair and get comfy, 'cause you're gonna want to stay for a while. Happy shadow-seeking!

Allison Dru Chabot, PhD
Media, Pennsylvania

Introduction

I've been afraid for most of my life. Afraid of the dark, afraid of situations that were seemingly scary, and afraid of my own shadow. The thought of travers- ing the unconscious mind to reexperience traumatic moments in my history was not something I would have signed up for just a few years ago. But then the unthinkable happened: I was diagnosed with cervi- cal cancer the week before my thirtieth birthday. The news came seemingly out of nowhere, and it shocked my doctors and me. I had no symptoms and few risk factors; yet cancer came anyway.

After my cancer diagnosis, I spiraled into a severe depression. I spent weeks alternating between crying and screaming, angry at the world that this was real, but angrier at myself because I believed that I was the reason it happened. I blamed myself because I had been ignoring the signs my body had been giving me suggesting that something was wrong, and instead just continued to push forward, focused on the next milestone I was attempting to reach. It took months to come out of that depression, and longer still to come to terms with what I had been through. The process aged me, drained me, and left me spinning, searching for an answer as to how this was possible.

My educational background is as licensed psycho-therapist. Having studied cognitive neuroscience and psychology throughout my career, I've spent my professional life trying to understand etiology. It's been my life's work to know why something happens and how to prevent it. And illness has always been an interesting topic for me, because there is so little that we know about how and why it originates. In fact, many illnesses (both mental and physical) don't have a known origin.

Over the years I have worked with clients with a range of sicknesses, from obsessive-compulsive disorder and borderline personality disorder to auto-immune disease and terminal illness. A question has always lingered in my mind—how can we diagnose and medicate someone for something we don't understand without trying to tackle the question of why it has presented itself in the first place? What if the answers we are seeking can't be found because we have been looking in the wrong place?

I began doing extensive research on the unconscious mind. During my search, I found that chronic stress is the number one cause of disease, including cancer, and I knew I had to start unpacking what unconscious material might have caused my body to create an environment where cancer could thrive.

Shadow Work is a book about using the power of the unconscious mind to unlock our potential. The shadow (also known as the unconscious) is a mechanism of the brain designed to repress information that is potentially too intense for the psyche. When it goes unchecked, the shadow builds up continually over time, creating a domino effect of negative consequences within the mind and body. And because this process is unconscious, it's hard to trace the consequences back to the root cause within the shadow. This unconscious material weighs us down and causes us to act out emotionally, behaviorally, and mentally. By entering the shadow, we can begin the healing work desperately needed to create coherence between all aspects of the self, allowing us to feel lighter, embodied, and free.

After practicing shadow work for several years, I made a discovery: *shadow work is the missing link in the manifestation process.* Manifestation is the practice of creating your future in your mind and then willing it to become your current reality. The present theory about manifestation is that you need to use all the sensory parts of your mind and body to create an environment where you welcome in the new reality that you seek. But what has been missing from this theory is the fact that most people are perpetually stuck in a trauma response hidden within the unconscious mind. When you remove the root cause of the trauma response, you truly open yourself up to experiences that may grant you access to what you are attempting to manifest. Once we have embraced, healed, and integrated the shadow, we can use the coherence that we have created to manifest *anything*.

That is why the shadow is so paralyzing. To begin to explore the shadow, we have to let go of the security blanket. We must drop the coping mechanisms and survival techniques we have been using for protection throughout our lives and hope that doing so will bring us to the next level of who we are meant to be.

The shadow is not scary. Though it sounds ominous, the shadow is a place of massive expansion and growth. Within the shadow is the truth about who you are, and endless possibilities for who you will become.

This book is for the people who are ready to release the security blanket because, even though it has helped them get this far, this isn't going to be their final destination. To reach the heights they are hoping to reach, they must be willing to step into the unknown—willingly, intentionally, and vulnerably.

No more running. No more hiding behind the security blanket. This is the moment to fully engage and brave the shadow to find out who you truly are.

Shadow Work is an invitation to no longer be *most* people, but instead become who *you* are meant to be on a soul level. And the journey begins now.

PART ONE

The Overlap of Science and Soul

"How can I be substantial without casting a shadow? I must have a dark side too if I am to be whole."
—CARL JUNG

1

Blast from the Past

In the fall of 2018, I had my first shadow work appointment with a renowned shadow worker in the United Kingdom named Allison Kelsey. I was fearful (maybe even terrified) of what I would experience during the appointment. At the time, I didn't even know what shadow work was. All I knew was that my gut was telling me that this practice was the missing piece of the puzzle in my healing journey, and I booked the first available appointment.

The session started very peacefully. Allison explained that we would need to achieve a very tranquil state in order to access my shadow, so the first few minutes began with a deep meditation. She instructed me to scan my body, relaxing into each area as we brought awareness to it. Beginning with the crown of my head, I focused my attention, noticing each little tingle or bit of tension that my body was experiencing. Having the focus on each part of my physical form permitted me to become fully embodied in the present moment, allowing any worries or fears that I may have carried with me to dissipate in an instant. I felt every bit of my body releasing any built-up tension that I had been holding onto, relaxing fully and easily.

Once I was visibly calm, Allison knew that my brainwave pattern had shifted, and thus our work could begin. She instructed me to use all of my senses, communicating with her anything that I might be seeing, hearing, feeling, smelling, and so on, as we embarked on our journey. She asked me to visualize staring down upon Earth from space as the world began to spin counterclockwise. I was shocked by how vivid this imagery was in my mind, the colors and sensory experiences so vibrant and tangible. When she felt it was time, Allison told me to see the Earth stop spinning and to begin floating down toward its surface.

During that first shadow work session, Allison took me to a past life in Scotland. When I landed on the Earth, I saw myself standing, feet in sandy rock, on a cliff overlooking a sapphire-colored ocean. I felt the temperature, which was quite cool for such a sunny day. The sky was a brilliant cerulean color with very few clouds. I felt the soft breeze on my skin, my heart pounding in my chest, and sensed overwhelming guilt and dread coursing throughout my body. The fear was surprising to me, because the place where I had landed was so beautiful, so serene—how could anyone feel dread in a place like this?

Allison asked me whether there was anything I needed to see in this past life, and my feet (which happened to be bare) immediately started moving in my mind's eye. I saw myself walking, one foot in front of the other, as my long, black, unkempt hair billowed around my face. I headed back away from the cliff's edge toward land, in the direction of a beautiful, lush forest. The deep green of the trees looked so enticing, but I had to keep moving. I turned around a corner away from the forest and began to make my way down the hill that was immediately next to the cliff I had just descended. I felt my knees wobbling as I walked and felt my breath catch in my chest as I tried to remain calm. Whatever it was that was causing me to feel this deep level of trepidation was nearby.

That was when I heard the shouting—angry screams echoing off the side of the cliff. It sounded like a mob of people, though I couldn't quite see them yet. The feeling of dread grew stronger as I followed the voices around the base of the cliff, circling down to a sandy beach. I felt a weight on my chest heavier than anything I had ever experienced, and I struggled to breathe, as if I were beginning to have a panic attack. That was when I saw them: a mob of angry villagers, dressed in garb that looked like it was from the seventeenth century. I couldn't believe it! My conscious mind was attempting to reconcile what I saw, trying to find any semblance of logic, but Allison told me to stay focused on just allowing the experience to unfold without trying to control it. Although this was easier said than done, I took a deep breath and refocused my attention on what was happening before me.

The villagers were roaring, raising their hands in the air, eagerly waiting for something to begin. And though I couldn't make out the majority of their words, I somehow knew their anger was directed toward me, that I was somehow the reason for this heightened level of emotion. I felt a knot in my throat the size of a baseball as I continued struggling to breathe, while Allison repeatedly assured me that I was safe. She brought my attention to my breathing pattern, which helped me to consciously and intentionally regulate my nervous system. I hung back from the crowd as best I could, not wanting to be noticed, but still able to observe the scene unfolding before me.

Suddenly, everyone's attention moved backward toward the woods as a young woman, bound at the wrists, was being dragged toward the mob by two large men. She looked as though she had been living in a hole for days; her clothes were ripped and dirty, her hair matted and caked with dried blood. Her eyes were sunken, as if she hadn't slept in weeks. When I saw her, a chill unlike anything I had ever experienced sent a shock wave through my body, and my blood ran cold. The young woman, who was wearing a simple tan dress that was covered in filth, looked at me with pleading eyes as she passed, while the crowd began to part to allow her captors to bring her to the front. Allison chimed in and asked me whether I understood what was happening here. Without thinking, I blurted out that we were about to witness the execution of a supposed witch. I had no idea where that information came from or why I said it, but I knew in my bones that it was true. It was as if I were watching a memory that I had long forgotten, and all of the information about this moment was still available in the recesses of my mind. The visuals and emotions were so crisp and vivid, the experience as tangible as if it had happened only yesterday. Allison then asked why the woman looked at me the way she did, with those sad eyes begging me to intervene. I once again responded immediately, stating that I was the one who was responsible for her death. That it wasn't her these villagers wanted—*it was me*.

In future appointments with Allison, she and I revisited this past life in Scotland several times to uncover more information about it. We needed to unearth why this lifetime had so much influence on my current one, and here is what we found: In this past life, I was the head witch of a coven of young women. I taught them herbalism, how to connect with and receive guidance from spirits, and how to help heal the sick. I was taught this information as an apprentice during my childhood and early teen years, before a fear of witches took hold in the coastal region of Scotland where I lived. I witnessed the moment when the tide began to turn, during a session in which I remembered giving a homemade doll to a child in town. When I gave the child the doll, the child's parents recoiled with fright. They believed I was trying to hurt the child with this gift; they claimed that I was consorting with the devil and that the doll I had bestowed on the child was evil. I felt the heartbreak of that moment in a way that felt so fresh, it could easily have just happened to me days ago in my current lifetime. I will never forget the look of sheer terror on the faces of those parents as we locked eyes in that moment.

Allison also helped me begin to put the pieces of the puzzle of that lifetime's importance together, recognizing that in that lifetime I had gone from being a sought-after healer in the local town, to a demonized outcast, to secret mentor, to ultimately losing everything during the witch trials, as the women who were in my coven were all killed one by one in an attempt to get me to leave town. In this past life, the local villagers were too afraid to target me; they thought I would put a curse on them and cause irrevocable harm to them and their families. In lieu of attacking me, they killed everyone I loved, leaving me completely alone with the unbearable guilt that their loss incurred. The final memory I saw from that lifetime was of taking my own life by jumping to my death from the cliff I had seen in my first past life visit. I witnessed myself slowly walking to the edge of the precipice, hearing the rumbling of the waves crashing down below. I felt myself take one final deep breath as I leaned over the edge and felt myself fall, and the relief I felt when it was over was astounding.

So why does this all matter?

What I discovered through my work with Allison is that hidden within our minds are memories that have been locked away. Our unconscious mind (also known as our shadow) houses information that our soul needs us to know but our brain is afraid to allow us to uncover. The reason this information is not readily accessible through the conscious is that the brain is unsure of how we will react to it. This potential instability triggers the mind to hide the information within the shadow until we are truly ready to access it. This hidden information dictates our personalities, our behaviors, and the lens through which we see the world. In short, our shadow makes us who we are, flaws and all. These unconscious memories come from a multitude of places, including our childhood and our past lives. Retrieving this information is easy, as all we need to do is access a specific brainwave state that allows unconscious information to readily pass through into the conscious mind. And when this unconscious material *isn't* conscious (as is true for most people), we are ruled by our shadow.

From reexperiencing that past life in Scotland, I was able to recognize that I have a few unconscious patterns that carried over into this lifetime:

1. I'm a loner. I tend to not let people get close to me, and this comes from a fear that the people closest to me will get hurt and I will be the one responsible.
2. I'm a natural-born teacher. I've been teaching people for lifetimes without any formal training, and I'm often offered teaching positions, including speaking for major universities like Thomas Jefferson University or educating as a professor at Penn State University's Brandywine campus, a position I kept for a number of years.

3. I have been afraid to speak about the mystical. With a background in psychology and cognitive neuroscience, I have found a safe haven in science. This is because, deep down, I felt that I needed this "normal" scientific information to keep me safe from the metaphorical angry mob.

When we visit unconscious memories and discover their impact, we're given the unique opportunity to heal from and entirely release the shadow that is keeping us from growing into the most aligned version of our soul. Throughout this book, I'll teach you everything you need to know about what shadow work is, what happens when we avoid the shadow, and how we self-sabotage our efforts to heal from unconscious memories; I'll also teach you how to use this information not only to return your mind, body, and spirit to baseline, but also to re-create your life on your terms.

Down the Rabbit Hole

Most people aren't determined to succeed. They have a dream, go in optimistically, face adversity, and then give up on the dream. When times get tough, it's easier to give up than it is to stay on the path of growth and expansion. But it's more than the fact that it's hard that holds them back. There are deep underlying processes at play within the mind and body designed to keep you at your current level, wherever that might be. Having a full understanding of those processes and how they operate internally will help you to overcome your own biology and hack the system designed to keep you stuck. When you become the master of your mind and body, possibilities become limitless, and a whole world of opportunity opens up for you. Having the life of your dreams is easier than you think, and throughout this book I am going to give you all the information and tools you need to begin living your dream life.

In section one, we will explore the three levels of consciousness to understand the role each one has in our cognition. We will also take a deep dive into learning about a specific mind-body process called the subconscious feedback loop that is responsible for the formation of our personality and behaviors. Once we grasp the subconscious feedback loop, we can understand how to alter aspects of ourselves to create opportunities for immense growth and success.

Next, we will learn about the shadow, or the unconscious mind, and the precise role that it plays in our world. I will explain how and why the brain decides to deposit memories into the shadow, and the significant impact these repressed memories have on our nervous system. I will also explain what shadow work is, including how to use it as a healing tool in your everyday life. Included are shadow work exercises that you can begin practicing immediately to start the process of making the unconscious conscious.

In section two, we will shift our focus to how to take power over the unconscious and subconscious processes that have been controlling your life. I'll explain the secret to success that I have seen with top entrepreneurs and thought leaders throughout the globe. You will learn who spirit guides are and discover how to connect with them during shadow work. I'll teach you about the role past lives and other things you'll uncover in your shadow play in your soul's journey, and how to use the rich information revealed to alter your current path. I'll also help you understand the psychology of self-sabotage, and how to override the automatic coping mechanism that is present in the mind and body.

In the third and final section of the book, we will pull all this information together to learn how to create change that lasts, using the power of shadow work and manifestation as a spiritual compass for creating the life of your dreams.

The most important thing you will ever do for yourself and your healing is to embrace your shadow and allow it to make you whole. If you have been feeling like there is more to you and to the life that you are meant to have but you haven't been able to pinpoint exactly what that is or how to find it, then *this is day one of the next chapter of your life*. This journey will take you to places you never imagined; and it all begins with a trip down the rabbit hole. . . .

2

Living on Repeat

Let's begin with the simple fact that we are all just brainwashed zombies experiencing our own version of Groundhog's Day. That may be a tough pill to swallow, but it is one that is universally true for all human beings. Each day we perform the same basic routines: wake up, scroll through our phones, go to the restroom and get ready, drink coffee, eat breakfast, and so on. Now this may not be quite the same as your morning, but it might be interesting to take a moment to think about what you do on a daily basis. Or if we were to ask the question in a different way: what is your consistent daily routine? What you will likely find is that your daily behaviors repeat every single day, every single week, every single year. And that's just the tip of the iceberg! Dr. Fred Luskin, a researcher from Stanford University, found that we repeat ninety percent of thoughts we have each day. *Ninety percent.* So if our behaviors are the same and our thoughts are the same, it is inevitable that our lives will be consistently the same.

This repetitive behavior is actually an evolutionary function of the brain. Our brains crave consistency for a very simple reason: consistency leads to known outcomes. There's nothing unpredictable about consistency, which is a relief for the brain because it takes less mental effort to experience the known. The unknown is full of daunting variables that could cause unknown reactions within the mind and body, so the brain does what it can to keep us on the current course. To understand how the brain does this, we first have to understand the different levels of consciousness.

Levels of Consciousness

Imagine an iceberg. In your mind, visualize the icy white mass floating above the water's surface. This portion of the iceberg is easily visible and readily accessible, subject to influence from the environment within its surroundings. The iceberg that floats above the water is akin to your conscious mind. The conscious mind is composed of the aspects of your cognition that you are fully aware of and able to influence. This includes things like what you ate for breakfast, who you are in a relationship with, whether you are going to go on a diet, and what book you are currently reading. Like the iceberg, this level of consciousness is fully within your scope of awareness.

Now envision the portion of the iceberg that is just below the water's surface but still visible to the eye. It may be a bit murky or distorted from the water, but it is still accessible enough that you can reach it if you need to. This level is analogous to the subconscious mind, which is the part of your cognition that controls automatic behaviors and thoughts. These functions that you experience automatically are ones that you are passively choosing, with little to no thought occurring as you do so. Examples of this are overeating, mindlessly scrolling through your phone, or habitual behaviors like driving to work without paying attention to where you're going—behaviors you engage in as if you're running on autopilot. When we consider Dr. Luskin's research about how ninety percent of our thoughts repeat every day, we can extrapolate that our daily life is primarily based on the subconscious.

But there is still one level deeper that we need to examine, and that is the portion of the iceberg that is so far below the water's surface that it is no longer visible to the naked eye. This section of the iceberg that lives within the depths of the water, hidden from sight, is similar to the unconscious mind. The unconscious is a collection of everything that has happened to you that the brain has hidden away out of reach. The brain might choose to hide information within the unconscious for many reasons, including trauma, and we will fully examine this topic later in the book.

According to the work of developmental biologist Dr. Bruce Lipton, author of *The Biology of Belief*, the subconscious controls ninety-five percent of our lives, while the conscious is in control of a mere five percent. Those numbers are startling, especially considering the extent to which we believe we are in full control of our own destiny. As it turns out, we are far more likely to remain the same than we are to change. And even more interesting is that Dr. Lipton discovered that seventy percent of our subconscious behaviors were acquired before the age of seven. Those subconscious behaviors originate from experiences that now live within the unconscious mind, long forgotten but ever present.

Let's break down what this means. Our lives are shaped by unconscious experiences that create our subconscious behaviors that we act out repeatedly each day. And when we make attempts to create conscious change within our lives, we often struggle because we don't understand how to alter subconscious behaviors. My belief is that we struggle to alter them because we're not actually getting to the source, which is the unconscious material that created the subconscious behavior in the first place.

The Subconscious Feedback Loop

It is imperative for our purposes that we understand how humans become brainwashed zombies walking around experiencing this thing called life, and that is through a function called the subconscious feedback loop. The subconscious feedback loop consists of four parts: experiences, chemical reactions, physical reactions, and thoughts. Each of these functions is part of the larger feedback loop that reinforces each aspect of the loop, ensuring that it will continue into the future.

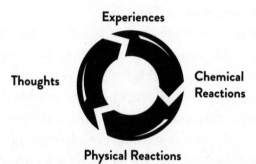

Experiences

Thoughts

Chemical Reactions

Physical Reactions

It all begins with an experience. Even before we are born, we are having experiences every moment of every day. And these experiences start the process of shaping our reality immediately by starting the chain reaction in the subconscious feedback loop. When we experience something, we use all of our senses to take in that information, hearing, seeing, smelling, and so on. The brain receives this information, and then it creates a chemical reaction to tell the body how to respond to the stimuli it just experienced. This chemical reaction sends a message to the body about how to respond to the experience appropriately, which creates a physical reaction. Blood and oxygen are pumped to particular areas to help the body navigate the experience. A signal is then sent back to the mind in the form of a thought, informing the mind how it should think about the experience that just occurred. This thought then signals the brain how this experience should be categorized, ensuring that the next time you experience a similar situation, you can replay this subconscious feedback loop and create a more streamlined process. As I mentioned earlier, the brain loves the known, so the more established subconscious feedback loops can be used, the better the brain likes it.

Here is an example of what this might look like: a four-year-old wakes up from his sleep and wants to find his mom and dad. He hops out of bed and opens his door, only to hear yelling downstairs. He tiptoes to the top of the stairs and sits down, listening to his mother and father in the midst of a heated argument. The child stays at the top of the staircase for a few minutes, continuing to listen to what is unfolding below, and then he eventually heads back to his room to go back to sleep.

The experience this child had was hearing the elevated voices of his parents with an argumentative undertone while being alone in a dark area. Because of his age, it is highly likely that the child didn't understand the context of the fight. Before the age of seven, children are egocentric, having a lot of difficulty seeing outside perspectives, so he probably assumed the yelling he heard from his parents was about him. This experience would have kickstarted the subconscious feedback loop chain reaction within his body, signaling the production of adrenaline and cortisol and causing them to begin to pump through the body. This process would have sent blood and oxygen to the areas of his body that would help him run, fight, or freeze, making his heart rate increase, his breathing get shallower, and even potentially causing him to have an upset stomach. It might also have caused him to choose to escape the situation by heading back to his room to get away from it. Then the thoughts that came up for him might have involved shame and guilt related to feelings of unworthiness, since the child made the egocentric assumption that he was the cause of his parents' fight.

Once this subconscious feedback loop is created, it is likely to repeat, as the brain can call upon this already formulated system to inform new experiences. Various trigger points could activate this subconscious feedback loop, including hearing people shouting, seeing displays of anger from others, being in the dark, or being alone and afraid. If this child were to encounter any of these variables in the future, this subconscious feedback loop could kick into gear, causing the child to spiral into negative behaviors or emotions.

Fast-forward to that same child becoming a twenty-five-year-old man who hears his boss yelling on the phone in his office. The experience from the past would inform the current experience, immediately causing the subconscious feedback loop to spring into action. The man's body would begin producing adrenaline and cortisol, which in turn cause blood and oxygen to rush to the same areas. The man feels the same need to run away, and he abruptly gets up from his desk to go into the hall. The same thoughts of shame and guilt around unworthiness would spring up, making him feel that he was the cause of the disturbance, an egocentric thought deeply embedded within his psyche arising from his original experience as a child.

As an outsider looking in, it's easy to assume that both the parents and the boss were yelling about things that had nothing to do with this person. But because the first experience was internalized this way, all experiences this boy/man has that follow and that are similar to the first one will be experienced similarly.

This subconscious pattern might be labeled anxiety by his doctors, and he would be treated with anti-anxiety medication to help alleviate the symptoms. But you and I both know that the root cause of the reaction he is experiencing is a forgotten memory within the unconscious mind. And breaking the initial subconscious feedback loop could alter the way he responds to situations like this for good.

Interrupting the Subconscious Feedback Loop

To create change, we need to learn how to stop the subconscious feedback loop in its tracks, and we can do this by simply interrupting the loop. Remember the four pieces of the subconscious feedback loop: experiences, chemical reactions, physical reactions, and thoughts. If we can cause an interruption at any one of these levels, then we can cause a disturbance in the loop that can cause it to break down.

For instance, if we can convince the man in our example that the sound of yelling is a neutral experience, fewer chemicals are likely to be released, which would mean there would be little to no physical reaction, and no thoughts would be necessary. Or if we were to interrupt on the level of thoughts, after he passed through the initial stages of the loop, we could tell him to do some mantra work and repeat words like "the yelling has nothing to do with me. I am at peace." If he continued to say (and mean) this repeatedly, his experience might change into one that was more relaxed, which would trigger the release of endorphins and signal the body to calm down and feel at ease. This sequence would reinforce the altered thought, potentially creating a new loop.

This sounds easy—so why isn't it? Mainly because it's hard to determine how to create the interruption without knowing the root cause of the loop's initial creation, which is hidden away within the unconscious mind. And that, my friends, is where shadow work begins.

Creating Coherence Within the Mind and Body

To practice shadow work, you have to begin to allow your mind and body to create coherence. This means allowing your entire energetic system to fall into alignment. The best way to achieve this alignment is through a regular meditation practice.

We'll begin with this meditation exercise:

Start by either lying or sitting in a comfortable position. For the purpose of this exercise, all you need to do is just be. Don't worry about focusing on anything specific, instead allowing whatever thoughts pop into your mind to enter. And when they do, gently allow them to leave.

Try this exercise for two to five minutes at first, and gradually increase your time. Doing this will allow you to access the unconscious mind more readily when we begin the shadow work process.

Note: If you feel resistance, that's okay! The limiting beliefs that pop into your head during this exercise are a coping mechanism of the brain, there to protect you from accessing the unconscious. Don't attempt to force them out, and don't be hard on yourself when they inevitably spring up. Just keep going, as this is the first step on your path to rewiring your mind and body.

Note: If you have difficulty allowing yourself to just be, you can incorporate gentle meditation music into your practice. This should only be temporary and be left behind once you become more comfortable meditating. Gradually decrease the volume of the music, and eventually remove it altogether. This is important because the music can be a distraction from the subconscious and unconscious thoughts that are attempting to bubble up to the surface. As long as the music is there, you might not reach the depths that your soul needs you to access.

The Science of Our Circuitry

Our brain consists of a series of "highways" known as neural pathways. This neural pathway system is the means by which messages are relayed throughout the brain and to the body, and these pathways are created by the subconscious feedback loop. Whenever we have a novel experience, a new neural pathway is laid down within the brain, so that if we have this experience in the future, a pathway has already been created. Over time, this neural pathway system becomes highly complex, wired in a way that is entirely unique to each person. The creation of each neural pathway is called *synaptogenesis*, and this process is an important part of our development. After the creation of a neural pathway, the subconscious feedback loop seeks to use these highways to confirm what it has already deemed to be true. And when these neural pathways are used often, they become more set within the mind.

To create space for new pathways, our brain sometimes seeks to remove older pathways that no longer serve us because we have not been using them. This process is called synaptic pruning and is a key piece of the process of shadow work. If we wish to change anything about ourselves or how we see the world, we need to create new neural pathways through synaptogenesis and use synaptic pruning to remove the ones our mind has been overusing and that are holding us back from growth and expansion.

Although synaptogenesis and synaptic pruning sound complex, they are processes that occur automatically in our brain. To hack this system, all we need to do is learn how to consistently interrupt the subconscious feedback loops that are no longer serving us; that will cause the neural pathways these loops use to be rendered unnecessary. While we are doing this, we need to replace the automatic subconscious feedback loops we are interrupting with new subconscious feedback loops that align with our desired version of reality. When we alter our experiences, our chemical reactions, our physical reactions, and our thoughts, we prompt the formation of new neural pathways that our brains can use instead, thereby encouraging rapid internal growth and expansion for ourselves on every level imaginable.

How We Self-Sabotage

The mind is hell-bent on keeping us safe, which is a clear survival mechanism of the brain. With our neural pathways laid out to rely on past experiences, the brain considers the known to be safe, and the unknown to be potentially threatening. To keep us from straying from the predictable known, the mind has a built-in mechanism to keep us stuck, known as *the ego*.

The ego is a term that was initially coined by Dr. Sigmund Freud. He described it as the inner voice of reason that mediates between our wants and desires. The ego is the voice inside your head urging you to stay small and not to stray from the path. The voice is often negative, using scare tactics, threats, or bullying to keep us on the straight-and-narrow path laid out before us. Our ego voices are also sometimes referred to as lower-limiting beliefs, because the ego voice tends to keep us stuck within a lower vibrational version of ourselves.

Think of the ego as the gatekeeper of your unconscious mind. Whenever you are close to uncovering unconscious material or interrupting the subconscious feedback loop, the voice of the ego will become louder and more intense as it attempts to move you back into complacency. This is why it is so important that we do shadow work: to quiet the voice of the ego for good, allowing us to continue to grow unchallenged by our own internal monologue.

3

Exploring
the Shadow

In my work as a psychotherapist, I consistently come across the same problem: my work with clients in the therapeutic setting would take them part of the way toward healing, but we couldn't *quite* reach the root of the issue they were seeking help for. And after a period of months or years, we would determine that this was as far as we were going to get, and we would part ways.

I've heard from hundreds of people that this was their personal experience of therapy as well. They have told me that therapy helped but they were unsure if it ever actually got to the heart of the issue they had entered treatment for. This situation never felt satisfying to me. I was sending people out of my office without having examined the moments that I knew had shaped their brains' wiring to form the loops they were currently battling, and that felt shallow and unrewarding. I knew I had to get to the root of the problem, but I wasn't sure where to begin—that is, until I needed to get to the root of my own issues.

On a cold December morning in 2018, I received a phone call from my doctor that completely altered the course of my life. I was sitting on my cozy black couch on a free morning—a rarity because of how busy my client schedule had been—gazing out the bay window of my Philadelphia row house. My home was on a quiet street, away from the hustle and bustle of the city center, which suited me fine, considering that my office was in the heart of the city. When I went in to see clients, I would regularly hear cars honking as they made their way around city hall, and sirens, or I'd swerve to avoid tourists taking photos in front of the Union League building. Having a small, cozy home within the city but tucked away from the noise was like having my own personal retreat. This day began more simply than most, as I sat in my flannel pajamas enjoying a warm cup of coffee, reflecting on the first twenty-nine years of my life. In just a few days, I would be thirty, a landmark moment in anyone's life. It was a seemingly perfect morning, until my phone rang.

I answered the phone to hear my doctor on the other end; she was clearly anxious to talk to me, as her tone seemed both apprehensive and stern. She was calling to tell me that I had cancer. *Cancer.* My entire world was flipped upside down in an instant. As she spoke, I was barely listening. It felt as though I had immediately slipped into a hazy fog, so although I could hear her words, not much was being processed. I brought myself back into consciousness a few moments later to hear my doctor stating adamantly that she couldn't determine the cause of my cancer. I had no symptoms, had very few risk factors, and was in good health. She let out a sigh and uttered, "Sometimes this just happens."

The next few months were a whirlwind of doctors' appointments, consultations, and surgeries. It all happened so fast, and I was swept up and carried off by the momentum of it all. I was simultaneously going through the motions while being completely dissociated from the experience, as if a robot had taken over to help me with the mechanics while my psyche ran away and hid from the process. My body was in shock from the experience, and I drifted into depression, which I believe arose mostly because I was faced with my own mortality for the first time. I lacked any control over the outcome, something I fervently resented, and there was nothing that I could do about it.

The final piece of my treatment was to undergo an open hysterectomy to remove the uterus, thereby preventing any spread (or potential spread) of the cancer. I was surprised by how overwhelmed I was by the idea of losing my womb. Although I had already had children, the reality that someone was taking away my ability to choose to bring more life into this world was like a nail in the coffin of my already fragile psyche, and I spiraled into the lowest place I have ever been in my entire life. I was crushed.

It took months for me to recover physically, mentally, and emotionally from cancer. And when I had done everything I could to deal with the symptoms, I fixated on the task of understanding why I had developed this sickness in the first place. And so I went to my psychology and cognitive neuroscience roots, researching articles and reading through textbooks until I stumbled upon a brief mention of the shadow. In that moment, something clicked within me, as if I knew the shadow was what I had been searching for. It was as if my entire life had led me there, and this was the work that I needed to do—not just for myself, but also for all the clients who were having trouble getting to the core issue that was causing them to seek help. I finally found the answer I had been searching for.

When I did my own shadow work, I realized that I had been unknowingly stuck in a trauma response for thirty years and didn't realize it until I began diving into the root cause of my cervical cancer. I had been frozen in a pattern whose origin I was unaware of, and this pattern was blocking my ability to live life on my terms. With shadow work, I was able not only to identify the root cause of my trauma response but also to completely free myself of it for good. Once the root had been eradicated, I learned to interrupt the subconscious feedback loops I was running and rewire my mind and body for health, ease, and abundance.

What Is the Shadow?

Carl Jung, a world-renowned Swiss psychiatrist, coined the term *shadow* in 1863, stating that it comprised the hidden aspects of the self. Jung believed that we repress deep within the psyche aspects of our personalities that we feel will be rejected, and that this repression causes imbalance within our minds, bodies, and spirits.

The shadow is another term for the unconscious mind, which, as you may remember from chapter two, is where the brain has hidden everything that has happened to you that could potentially be disruptive to keep it out of reach. Hidden deep within, buried underneath layers that feel impenetrable, the shadow is kept at bay—at least for a time.

Someone might have memories stored within the shadow for any number of reasons; it could be because of the negative emotions surrounding an experience, such as shame, guilt, sadness, or anger. It could be because they experienced extreme physical or mental pain, and the mind deemed the trauma too much to handle consciously. It could be because it doesn't fit the narrative that family, society, or media has projected onto them. And there are other times when information just finds its way there at random.

When information is stored within the shadow, it is still accessible to us. But it becomes much harder to reach as a result of the unconscious "safety net" that keeps the mind and body in a state of homeostasis. The mind strives for consistency, and the hidden shadow material within the unconscious mind could potentially disrupt the consistent landscape of the conscious mind.

Think of all of the times in your life when you have felt utterly stuck. Maybe it was when you celebrated a milestone birthday that reminded you that you thought life would be different by now. Perhaps it was when you had an epiphany that your current career trajectory was not what you expected, but you were unsure how to pivot. It may have concerned a relationship, when you woke up next to your partner thinking *how did we get here?*

That stuck feeling arises when you need to access information from the unconscious, but your mind and body won't allow you to go there. So you can't get to the root of *why* you feel stuck, and you may feel hopeless and trapped in your attempts to work through whatever is causing you to feel stuck in the first place.

Over time, shadow information builds up and overwhelms the mind's delicate balance, and when this happens, illness and disease are created within the mind and body. Mental illnesses such as anxiety and depression are indicators that the shadow is overflowing into other levels of consciousness, interrupting thought patterns and sleep cycles. But without shadow work to access the root cause of the overflow, the symptoms worsen over time, potentially leading to more severe illnesses.

The purpose of shadow work is to make the unconscious conscious. It's imperative to understand and heal the unconscious processes that are causing you to feel trapped within your own mind and body. And although the term *shadow* may sound intimidating, the shadow is something that most of us actively seek without realizing it. We romanticize the notion of finding ourselves, and we crave the depth of connection that comes from having profound, loving relationships with others. Shadow work is the process of creating that depth within and lovingly accepting all parts of yourself. And when you can finally look at the things you have hidden away, you can release the shadows and integrate them, making yourself healthier and more whole than you could have imagined.

Shadow work will make it possible for you to interrupt the subconscious feedback loops that are keeping you stuck. Then you can replace them with opportunities to change your life for good.

Shadow Work Meditation and Journaling

Create a quiet, comfy, uninterruptable space (turn off the phone, lock the doors, and so on). Have a journal and a pen handy and any other tools that will help you deepen this experience, such as dim lighting, crystals, candles, comfortable clothing, or oils.

For a few minutes, allow your mind to go quiet. Let everything you were thinking about before you sat down be released as you focus on your breath. Take long inhales in through the nose, and breathe long exhales out through the mouth. Imagine that the air you are breathing in is beautiful, white light energy, and that the air that you exhale is gray smoke carrying heavy energy out and away from your energetic system. As you breathe, bring your awareness into your body. Think about how your body feels, starting at the crown of your head and working your way down to the bottom of your feet. Once you are fully present and in your body, ask yourself the following questions:

- What is my biggest fear in life?
- Where did this fear come from?
- How am I perpetuating that fear?
- What can I do to release that fear?

Allow the voice of your inner guidance system to speak through you, and don't question the answers that come through. After you ask each question, record the answer in your journal. Just allow yourself to write without thinking, which will create a stream of consciousness.

Note: This exercise is designed to help you access unconscious thoughts to bring them into your conscious awareness. If the brain is attempting to block these messages from coming through, it's because your built-in safety protocol defenses are still up and active—that means you're not relaxed enough yet. Start the body scan section of the exercise over, and focus on your breath as you do. Allow any tension or stress to melt away and move through the exercise slowly. When you're done, ask those questions again. And remember, those defense mechanisms have been in place for most of your life. Practicing this until those defense mechanisms release is essential, and it may take a few tries before you start receiving answers.

Note: Once you have had those questions answered, think about other things you wish to know about yourself. You can ask why you're stuck, how that happened, how you perpetuate feelings of being stuck, how being stuck is serving you, and so on. The possibilities are endless. Make a list of questions to ask yourself during your next shadow work meditation and journaling session.

4
What Happens When We Repress?

When I was in my first year of graduate school, studying to become a psychotherapist, one of my professors asked my cohort a simple question: what was it that messed us up so badly that we needed to try to fix it by becoming a therapist? I was utterly shocked by this question. I thought to myself, *nothing messed me up, of course!* My life was perfect! I had fantastic grades in graduate school, I came from a loving family, I had close friendships and a supportive partner. How could someone insinuate that I was using this profession to fill a void in my healing?

Years later, I realized how right that professor was. Becoming a psychotherapist was just another example of repressing my traumas while using the healing of others as a mask for those traumas. And the thing that messed me up so badly that I needed to become a therapist to fix it was my need for *control.*

In the cognitive neuroscience world, there is ample research and evidence that the brain wires itself in patterns. Neural pathways, the brain's wiring system, are created around our earliest memories. And these early memories set the stage for what I like to call our *life lens,* or the way in which we see the world. Once the earliest neural pathways are laid, the brain seeks experiences and information that will reinforce what it has already deemed to be true; that way, it can expand on the neuronal networks (neural pathway systems) that already exist. That also means the brain disregards information that doesn't fit into the neural pathways it's currently using.

When this occurs throughout our lifespan, our life lens becomes very narrow and specific, and creating change becomes increasingly more difficult. By age twenty-five, it may almost feel like your point of view is hardwired. Various theories within the psychotherapy framework reiterate this construct, each suggesting in slightly different ways that we each have a core conflict we struggle with that begins in our neural wiring. And these core conflicts shape the relationships we choose throughout our lifetime.

Simplified, our life lenses are those through which we see the world. Identifying your life lens can help you understand how your brain has wired itself and provide a window into the underlying issues that created this life lens in the first place.

Discover Your Life Lens

Which feels most important to you?

1. Creating a life of freedom, where you can choose to live on your own terms.
2. Having control over your life; feeling like you are in the driver's seat at all times.
3. Making sure that things are fair and equitable for you and those around you.
4. Feeling powerful in your life and career choices.
5. Needing to feel safe and secure in your life and in your body.

Which of these would make you feel the worst?

1. Being stuck in a career path that doesn't fulfill you or allow you to pursue hobbies.
2. Someone trying to tell you how to do something or how to live your life.
3. Witnessing injustices against yourself or others and not being able to do anything about it.
4. Watching others rise up above you as you remain stuck behind.
5. Feeling helpless or hopeless in your life or your body.

Your life lens based on your answers:

1. Freedom
2. Control
3. Fairness
4. Power
5. Safety

Note: You may feel like more than one of these apply to you. To get clarity on which life lens you view the world with, take some time to journal about how these may fit (or not fit) into your life until you find the one that is the best fit.

Note: These life lenses are based on my decade of work as a psychotherapist, but you may find that there is another lens that suits you better. Find the word that causes a reaction in your body, even if it's not on this list. Find the one that gives you an "aha moment," and trust that that is your life lens!

Your life lens is the viewpoint through which you see the world, and it began to take shape at the beginning of your life. It's highly likely that early, repressed traumas have influenced the formation of the life lens. Every experience you have either reinforces or challenges your life lens, and early traumas are no different.

Understanding Trauma

In early 2019, I underwent a hysterectomy. The goal was to ensure that if there were any cancer cells left, they would be removed from my body completely to preclude further spreading or recurrence of cancer later in my life. My doctor insisted that, instead of less-invasive measures, she should perform an abdominal hysterectomy, meaning that she would make a six-to-seven-inch incision in my lower abdomen to enable her to remove my uterus. This was a last-minute decision that was made only two days before my surgery, and I didn't have much time to grapple with it. I chose to trust my doctor and move forward with her plan.

On the morning of the surgery, my parents drove down to Philadelphia from New York, and both they and my husband accompanied me to the hospital. I was much more nervous than I had anticipated being, mainly because something felt *off*. Energetically, spiritually, I had a feeling that the energy wasn't right, and it was making me rethink the whole endeavor. Against my better judgment (and mainly because I didn't feel like going through the build-up to surgery again at a later date), I stayed. Hours of waiting were finally over when I was called back into surgery prep, my mother accompanying me until it was time for anesthesia. When we bade each other goodbye, she told me that everything was going to be fine and she would be there when I awoke. The surgery was a success, and I was wheeled into a recovery wing to allow me to wake up from anesthesia under the supervision of a medical professional.

However, when I began to wake, I felt physically paralyzed. I was completely lucid and could still feel excruciating pain despite the paralysis, but I was entirely unable to move or speak. I could see the nurse right in front of me, her brown hair pulled into a sleek bun at the nape of her neck, as she sat with her legs crossed, staring at a computer a mere ten feet from me.

But she wasn't looking in my direction, no matter how hard I tried to will her to do so. I was more terrified than I had ever been in my entire life. While I lay there in an anesthesia-fueled paralysis, I could feel myself going into shock. My anxiety skyrocketed, my breathing became extremely shallow, I looked down with my peripheral vision and observed that my skin was pale and gray, and I felt dizzy and nauseated from the pain. This lasted for what felt like an eternity but realistically was most likely around twenty minutes. Eventually my mouth began to allow small movements, so I tried to move my mouth enough to form the word *help*. It took a few minutes of my feeble attempts to cry out for the nurse to notice and come to my aid, and then she assumed I needed more pain medication and upped my dose to allow my body some comfort. She didn't understand that what I was asking for was not help with the pain, but help with the paralysis. But once more medication made its way into my system, I drifted back into a deep sleep.

When I was finally awake again and able to move, I was absolutely shaken from the experience I had just had. As if the surgery itself hadn't been traumatic enough, anesthesia-fueled paralysis unquestionably took it over the edge. I was in a world of pain, more than I could have ever anticipated presurgery, and I was more afraid than I had ever been in my life. After this horrific experience, I couldn't wait to be reunited with my husband and parents, to have them hold me, reassure me, and tell me everything was going to be all right.

But when the nurse wheeled my bed down the hall and we arrived outside the door of my hospital room, only my husband stood there. Wearing a brown jacket and jeans, and with a with a dejected look on his face, he let me know my parents had left. It was at this moment that I broke down completely.

Big "T" and Little "t" Trauma

When we think about trauma, we often imagine disturbing events, such as watching people die on a battlefield or surviving horrific natural disasters. But trauma can be defined as any distressing experience, and the level of that distress can vary greatly among people and incidents. This is extremely important for shadow work, because *any* occurrence that causes significant distress could cause the mind and body to repress the incident, no matter what that event might be.

Traumas are broken down into two categories: big "T" trauma and little "t" trauma. Big "T" traumas are those that are deeply disturbing and/or life-threatening; they can often lead to a diagnosis of post-traumatic stress disorder, or PTSD. Examples of events that might cause PTSD are finding the body of someone who has committed suicide, waking up in the middle of surgery, or losing a child. Little "t" traumas are ones that affect you intensely but are not necessarily life-threatening or overtly disturbing. Examples of little "t" traumas are finding out your significant other has been having an affair, being bullied by a classmate or co-worker, or losing a parent suddenly.

When we experience any kind of trauma, the subconscious feedback loop kicks in. The experience triggers a chemical reaction, which communicates to the body how it should respond, which in turn informs the brain how it should think. This subconscious feedback loop can create or reinforce neural pathways.

Trauma is different from other experiences in that the brain and body can't disregard it if it doesn't fit the brain's neuronal network. Trauma will only reinforce what the brain already knows by giving it a more concrete foundation, or it will create a neural pathway that branches off from an existing one. The other way trauma is different is that the brain works to actively repress traumas within the unconscious mind. This is an evolutionary feature of the brain, meant to keep us safe. Think about what life would be like if you were actively thinking about your traumas every single day. You would likely fall into a deep depression and maybe even lose your will to live. Repressing traumas means the neural pathways are still there but the root source is hidden, enabling you to keep moving forward in a way that makes the psyche less fragile.

How Trauma Is Stored

As mentioned earlier, the mind is constantly sorting experiences to determine how best to use them. Some go into the conscious, others into the subconscious, and most into the unconscious. And very often, trauma is stored in the unconscious because the brain is unsure how keeping the event within the conscious mind would affect us.

Unfortunately, the body does not have the same capability of being able to sort information, and all physical memories remain fully present. This is why our bodies respond intensely to moments that are reminiscent of past traumas. When we experience anything that resembles a traumatic moment, our bodies immediately kick us into a fight/flight/freeze response, which activates our subconscious feed-back loop. The stimuli that kick off this response are referred to as triggers, and triggers create a response any time the body is given an indication that there is a potential for retraumatization. A common example of a trauma trigger is when war veterans are activated by fireworks or ceiling fans. Their bodies are unable to differentiate between real and imagined threats, so they perceive fireworks and gunshots similarly, just as they experience ceiling fans and helicopter blades in a similar way. Those triggers will activate the subcon-scious feedback loop, causing the body to activate the fight/flight/freeze response. These experiences (how-ever benign they might be) will reinforce the neural pathways that have already been laid down for the original trauma, ensuring that they continue to repeat whenever a trigger presents itself.

When someone experiences trauma, the mind can repress it, but the trauma remains active in the body. The physical reaction to the trauma is still present and prepared to be activated if a trigger presents itself.

For instance, if as a young child you were abused by a parent every night at about midnight, you might forget the trauma but still have immense difficulty sleeping. Your body might be on high alert, reacting as if the threat of abuse were still present, even if the abuse hasn't happened in years and the abuser is no longer present.

As you go about your daily life, you might find yourself being triggered by things that resemble the trauma you experienced but be unable to readily locate the source. Your body might remain activated while your mind represses the reason that this is occurring. This dynamic can lead to issues in your personal life as you become triggered. The resulting reaction can cause you to lash out or run away without knowing why you're experiencing such emotions. Furthermore, those around you might be confused by your behavior, as the trigger that is activating you might have absolutely no effect them. Furthermore, depending on how you are affected by your traumas, you may even find that you have trouble creating stable relationships in the first place and that you push friends, family, and potential partners away without having a true understanding of what is going on within you to cause that automatic reaction.

Our shadow rules us because it shapes our brains, alters our worldview, affects our bodily functions, and dictates our behaviors, *all without our knowing what the root cause is.*

Trust Your Body

Just as our bodies hold all of the information about our traumas, they also have innate wisdom and understanding about our wants and desires. Although we typically rely on conscious thoughts to help us discern which choices to make during our decision-making process, it is our bodies that we should defer to for guidance.

Within the gastrointestinal tract are millions of nerve cells that make up what is referred to as the enteric nervous system (ENS). The ENS is primarily responsible for issues related to digestion; however, it was recently discovered that is has a direct impact on our minds as well. The ENS influences our mood and our thoughts, creating a reciprocal loop between the mind and the body. In fact, the ENS is the bodily system responsible for the physical reaction to thought in our subconscious feedback loop. If you have ever gotten a gut feeling about a certain situation or person, you can bet that it was the ENS giving you that heightened awareness.

Because our bodies house the physical information for all of our memories (no matter which level of consciousness they exist on), our bodies remember everything we experience. Any moment from your life, traumatic or not, is still fresh in the awareness of the physical body. If there is a choice to be made, the body can inform you of the best course of action based on *all* your collective experiences, because the body remembers each one of them completely.

There is a reason we are told to trust our gut; our ENS is acutely aware of everything we should consider during the decision-making process. And our logical minds aren't privy to all of the information required to make a solid choice. Below, I have detailed an exercise called the human pendulum technique to help you tap into your body's innate wisdom whenever you need to make a decision.

The Human Pendulum

Try this exercise to tap into your body's innate wisdom, and allow yourself to begin incorporating it into your regular decision-making process. Use it whenever you need answers to yes-or-no questions.

Begin by drinking a large glass of water to fully hydrate the body. Don't skip this step—the water in your body is what enables the human pendulum to move, so you need to be properly hydrated for this task.

In a moment, you will begin asking yes-or-no questions out loud and noticing how your body reacts. Your body will move in one of four directions: forward, back, left, or right. Every person is different, so you will need to find out which direction your body moves in for yes and which direction it moves in for no.

Stand with your feet hip-width apart and keep your hands down at your sides. Calibrate your human pendulum by asking the following questions that you know the answers to:

1. Is my name _____?
   (For example, is my name Danielle?)
   Notice which direction you move in for yes.
2. Is my name Mother Goose?
   Notice which direction you move in for no.
3. Am I currently living in
   _____?

   Notice which direction you move in for yes.
4. Am I currently living on Mars?
   Notice which direction you move in for no.

Now that you have your human pendulum calibrated, feel free to ask yourself any question that you desire a yes or no answer to, and see which way your body moves after you ask. With this technique, you'll receive definitive answers that you can trust because they come from your body's own inner wisdom.

Here are some sample questions:

- Am I currently in the right career?
- Is my relationship serving me?
- Am I allergic to gluten?
- Do I have unconscious memories weighing me down?
- Are the steps I'm taking for my health enough?
- Am I getting enough sleep?

The possibilities are endless. I often use this technique for questions as small as what foods my body needs, or as big as whether I should write a book about shadow work. Your body always has the answers, and this is a wonderful way of learning how to listen.

Note: If your body isn't moving, you are probably dehydrated. Drink another glass of water and wait five minutes before trying again.

Repression and the Split

We have been taught that there is a great divide throughout our world. Us versus them, black versus white, light versus dark. Duality is an idea that has been around for centuries and makes for excellent story-telling. In movies and television shows, the hero conquers the villain and love always wins. The media often magnify the negative aspects of the psyches of those who have been deemed bad. As children, we are told by parents and teachers that we are either a good child or a bad child, and shame and guilt begin to take hold of us early in life. But what if the concept of duality was a construct that was helping to keep us stuck? In fact, what if duality itself makes the dark aspects of us even darker?

Think about repressing the urge to eat a treat. In your mind, you have to remind yourself of all the reasons the treat is bad. Maybe you tell yourself the effects it will have on your physical body, or how you will feel emotionally after you have eaten it. What you are attempting to do is to repress your natural physical urges. And when something feels off-limits or forbidden, the desire for it grows.

If you were to approach this situation from a neutral standpoint, the entire situation would flow very differently. You might decide to have a bite. Maybe it's delicious, and you have a second. When you feel satiated, you would push the plate away feeling happy and at peace. No psychological bullying, no beating yourself up, no demonizing yourself or the treat. The mind would not be at war with itself, intent on beating the bad child out of it.

For human beings, duality is completely embedded into the psyche, acting as a universal lens through which we see the world. We categorize everything into opposing camps, including the food we eat, the media we engage with, the people in our lives, and even our own behaviors. And this is exactly why we repress the darker aspects of ourselves: out of fear that we will realize that we are "bad."

But if we approached ourselves from a neutral standpoint, there would be no reason to repress, as all aspects of the self would be welcome. We would own every part of our behaviors and personalities, instead of fighting against them in a continually losing battle. No one would define themselves as good or bad. They would simply be well-rounded human beings having a human experience, which naturally has highs and lows but more often exists somewhere in between. We would lose the all-or-nothing mentality that is holding us back from inner peace.

Since we have been taught duality from the time we were young children, with parents telling us that we were either a good child or a bad child, duality is quite literally embedded into our minds. Our brains are wired to repress the unwanted aspects of the self, rather than embracing them as pieces that make us whole. We all have darkness. We all have impulses, desires, and things that we enjoy that others might not. But encouraging duality in our external world and creating a split within the psyche have created the basis for many mental and physical illnesses that we struggle with.

This is something that is easily seen in people who struggle with addiction. In their attempts to be "good," they are repressing the traits that would make themselves or others define them as "bad." We know from the earlier example that when we repress the darker parts of ourselves, it only makes them stronger. The addict is in a constant battle based on duality, trying to hide their impulses, yet these desires keep bubbling up to the surface. And when this happens consistently over time, the darkness eventually wins out.

What we are experiencing when this happens is an example of two subconscious feedback loops in action. When an addict gives in to their addiction, their early experiences of the addiction have informed their mind to activate the reward pathway in the brain. This pathway consists of the mesolimbic dopamine pathway, which includes ventral tegmental area (VTA) and the nucleus accumbens (NAc). This pathway informs the brain when something is highly pleasurable, activating other areas of the brain to remember to repeat this behavior in the future so that it can experience the reward again. This chemical reaction in the brain simultaneously activates the subconscious feedback loop by creating emotional, physical, and thought-based reactions to the experience, further ensuring that it repeats itself in the future.

There's a concurrent subconscious feedback loop happening as well, activating shame and guilt. The addict's early experiences of being "bad" cause the brain to trigger the fight/flight/freeze response, releasing chemicals like adrenaline and cortisol. These chemicals create a reaction in the body, making breathing shallower, causing blood to rush to the extremities, and activating brain fog. This sends an ego-message back up to the mind as well, reinforcing that, yes, this is a shameful, guilt-ridden act, making it more likely that this subconscious feedback loop will be activated in the future.

The experience of indulging in an addiction is a dual experience itself. Many addicts think to themselves: *if this addiction is so wrong, then why does it feel so right?* The dissonance experienced in the mind and the body can be completely overwhelming, and addicts have an incredibly difficult time quitting their addiction because of it.

You see, everything about the world as we know it would change if we weren't taught to engage in duality. If every aspect of the self were welcome, without a judgment about whether it belonged in one box or another, we would undoubtedly see a lot less polarized behavior on a collective level. The brain wouldn't re-create moments of simultaneous excitement and shame because there would be no need; without judgment, these dual subconscious feedbacks loops wouldn't need to exist together any longer.

This is why shadow work is the most important thing you can do for your well-being. When we integrate the shadow, there is a total acceptance of every aspect of the self. We begin to understand what makes us who we are, and we rewire the neurological pathways that have caused judgment-based reactions to our shadow selves in the past. And because we're not repressing aspects of the self, there's less stress on the mind and body, allowing our minds and bodies to function appropriately and focus their efforts wherever they are needed, rather than being overtaxed and working to stop the impact of chronic stress.

Challenge Duality

Grab a journal and a pen, and draw a line down the center of the page. On the top of the left side, write the word "good." On the top of the right side, write the word "bad." Close your eyes and ask yourself: *What things do I allow to fall into duality? What do I consider to be good or bad?* Open your eyes and begin to write down everything that falls into those categories.

Once you have your list, pick any pair of opposing ideas and write a journal entry about why they're *not* all good and bad. For example, if you believe criminals are bad, come up with examples that negate that idea within your mind, such as the fact that many incarcerated criminals are wrongly accused, or many are considered criminals for non-violent, petty crimes that are not necessarily bad.

The goal of this exercise is to help your mind shift you away from duality into a more integrated and holistic perspective. Repeat this exercise daily to challenge your automatic thoughts and shift your brain's neural pathways.

EXAMPLE:

Good	Bad
Healthy foods	Unhealthy foods
Reading books	Watching television
Working hard	Resting

SAMPLE JOURNAL ENTRY ABOUT HEALTHY AND UNHEALTHY FOOD:

Though I have been led to believe that I should always choose to eat healthy foods such as fresh fruit and vegetables, this does not inherently mean that unhealthy foods are bad. For example, food can have a component that links it to memory, so although pasta is not a healthy food, I have wonderful memories of my grandmother cooking pasta for large family dinners on Sundays throughout my life. The gathering of family and the love and warmth we felt toward each other are inherently connected to these shared Sunday meals. For that

reason, I can happily allow myself to pair this ste-
reotypically unhealthy food with a reason it belongs
in the "good" category and help my mind release
the idea that any food is entirely good or bad.

Challenging duality and allowing yourself to embrace every aspect of who you are is the cornerstone of shadow work. By integrating every facet of who you are and releasing any negative emotions that you have paired with the "less-desirable" aspects of yourself, you can truly see the beauty in every piece of your being. And there is no gift more valuable than the gift of complete and utter self-love and acceptance.

PART TWO

The Journey to Self

5

The Secret of Success

Life in this day and age is all about chaos. Global news leaves us worried about things that are out of our control, making us fear for our future because of things that we will probably never encounter. We have religion, which makes us feel shame for our thoughts, our impulses, and our past, causing us to feel collective internal dissonance. We live in a culture of materialism, a product of social media and television shows that make us feel the need to constantly give our energy away by consuming resources. We have technology readily at our fingertips, causing us to dissociate from our reality as we indulge in someone else's. There is government, asserting control over the masses while also instilling fear and confusion because the rules are ever-changing. And there is the rising cost of living, causing people to earn less, work more, and numb their worry away.

It's no wonder that we, as a collective, feel more disconnected now than ever. The past forty years or so have been a build-up to this moment, when mental and physical health problems are at an all-time high and quality of life is at an all-time low. Chronic stress, the number one cause of all disease, both mental and physical, is also at an alarming high. In fact, in a study conducted by the American Psychological Association, seventy-seven percent of people polled reported having physical symptoms as a result of chronic stress occurring in the month they were polled.

From doing shadow work, I can see quite clearly that we are not meant to live like this. We are like hamsters on a wheel that only get off the wheel when some major health issue occurs that forces us off, very often because it leads to death. As much as we don't want to live life this way, it can be difficult to find a way off the wheel when the wheel itself is the status quo.

Chronic stress is the result of an overactive autonomic nervous system, and it can lead to anxiety and depression. Anxiety is worry about the future, while depression is rumination on the past; so whichever you are diagnosed with is an indicator of how your neural pathways have formed. Both anxiety and depression serve a unique purpose: to block us from being able to connect to the moment that we are currently in, which keeps us stuck in our subconscious feedback loops.

One of the ways you can begin to break this pattern is to become more consciously aware of the present moment. This is incredibly simple to do; all you need to do is take a step back and notice what is happening both in and around you right now, with no distractions pulling your attention away. You can bring your attention to your senses, noticing what you are experiencing in the moment. Listening to the noises in your immediate surroundings, taking a deep breath in and noticing what the air smells like, and feeling whatever parts of your body are touching things, whether the ground, a chair, or something else. In its simplest form, this is meditation: a full mental, physical, and emotional attachment to the moment you are currently experiencing.

When we step away from the chaos that surrounds us, we are interrupting a deeply embedded subconscious feedback loop that is reinforced from all angles. And though it may take some time to cause this neuronal network to deteriorate since it is so highly reinforced, baby steps will help you begin to erode it slowly over time. Repetition is key in this process, and daily meditation, no matter how quick the meditation might be, will help too.

We tend to complicate meditation, thinking it is something that only elite people who have the luxury of turning their minds off are capable of doing. In fact, thinking about meditation might conjure up images in your mind of Buddhist monks in their tranquil monasteries, or rich Manhattan socialites whose nannies bear the brunt of the childcare and housekeeping responsibilities so that they are free to meditate whenever they please. But in fact, meditation is easier and more accessible than you think once you broaden your definition of what meditation is.

Meditation can be defined as a period of quiet reflection and mental engagement in an effort to achieve heightened levels of spiritual connection. Although that definition may play into any preconceived notions that you have about how meditation is performed, here are some things to consider.

- ○ **NOT ALL MEDITATION IS PERFORMED WITH YOUR EYES CLOSED:** Connecting to your inner self doesn't require your eyes to be shut for you to reach heightened levels of awareness.

- ○ **YOU DON'T NEED TO BE SITTING DOWN TO MEDITATE:** Although one of the most popular ways to meditate is from a seated position, you can just as easily do meditations while on the go. These are referred to as walking meditations, and they are becoming increasingly popular.

- ○ **SILENCE IS NOT REQUIRED FOR MEDITATION:** Feel free to meditate while listening to soft music, allowing yourself to fully engage with the frequency of the sounds that you are tuning in to. Let them guide you inward so that you can quiet the noise of the world around you and focus on the present.

- **MEDITATION IS NOT ABOUT CLEARING YOUR MIND:** We've all heard the notion that meditation is about completely clearing your mind of thought, allowing any passing ideas to float away rather than letting them linger. But what if those thoughts are showing up for a reason? Instead of feeling overwhelmed by their presence, ask them in a nonjudgmental manner what they are there to show you.
- **MEDITATION CAN BE SHORT AND SWEET:** Although some meditation sessions can be quite lengthy, they don't have to be! Stay in the present moment for as long as you feel called to, and gently bring yourself out of it whenever you choose. You are in control of the process.

Bringing your awareness to the here and now is one of the best forms of meditation, as it completely aligns you with your current reality. Doing this releases you from the chokehold all the above-mentioned distractions have on your mental, physical, and emotional well-being, bringing you to a state of overall peace and tranquility, even if it's only for a short time. Continuing to practice meditation regularly will help alter your body and mind's natural state because you will be interrupting the previously operating subconscious feedback loops that you had been employing, giving space for new, more aligned ones to emerge and set you free.

Simple Meditation to Bring Awareness to the Present Moment

This meditation can be done at any moment, no matter where you are.

Find somewhere comfortable to sit. Bring your awareness to your breath, noticing how it feels when it makes its way in through your nose, gently gliding along your palate, down the back of your throat, and down toward your lungs. Feel your chest and belly expand as you make space for that air and notice how it feels. Is the air that you're breathing in cold or warm? What does the air smell like as you breathe it in?

Let out a big exhale through your mouth and notice how the air feels traveling back up through your throat and out of your mouth. What is the temperature like? How do your chest and belly react as you release this air?

Notice any pain, tension, or tightness in your physical body. Wherever you feel it, take a moment to stretch or rub that spot, releasing the energy that you're holding in this physical location and allowing it to leave your body.

What is one beautiful thing that you see in your immediate surroundings? Is it a small rain droplet on a leaf, something so insignificant you might not have noticed it before? Or maybe the smile of someone in your immediate vicinity, their light radiating off them in this moment? Maybe it's your cozy bedroom, the safe haven you have created for

> yourself that continues to make you feel warm and protected. Notice the beauty that exists all around you in every moment, each day, no matter how small.
>
> Stay here for as long as you like.

Meditation is an integral piece in the process of shadow work because it allows you to become more than the embodiment of the subconscious feedback loops that control you. It releases you from your past and your future fears, allowing you to be fully present so that you can journey inward without interruption.

When you become proficient at this practice, you can up the ante by closing your eyes. Removing your sense of sight will heighten your other senses and allow your mind's eye to take over as your primary visual vehicle. It is from this place that much of your future shadow work will be done.

The Time I Accidentally Manifested My Dream Home

When my youngest was nearing one year old, I began longing for a new home. The small row home my family and I occupied in South Philadelphia was much too small for our newly created family of four, and it often felt like the walls were closing in on us. Toys were overflowing from every corner of the house, the kitchen cabinets could no longer house all of our dishes and cups, and the claustrophobia my husband and I felt was overwhelming.

At the time, I was working as an adjunct professor at Penn State University's Brandywine campus, teaching a few classes in the psychology department. During my breaks I would pore over housing websites, ogling different modestly priced homes in the area, wishing we could afford them but knowing they were out of our reach. With my meager income as an adjunct and my small psychotherapy practice, I couldn't help ease the burdens of the bills we currently had, let alone add a large mortgage payment.

It was around this time that I began practicing shadow work. I spent my weeks diving into my traumas, scouring through my past to remove negative attachments that I was repressing to allow them to heal completely. I also added a kundalini yoga practice in addition to daily meditation, where I allowed my mind to roam freely, completely uninterrupted. In doing so, I noticed that my outlook on my current home began to change. I stopped feeling connected to the negative emotions that I had associated with my current home, instead feeling intense gratitude for all the wonderful things that home had done for us. It gave us shelter, warmth, the ability to be close to my husband's family, and years of memories with my husband and young children (all their firsts had happened in that house!). When I was able to detach from the past and live in the present, something shifted within me. For the first time, I was no longer living based on my past, but instead focusing all my attention on the present moment.

When I was firmly committed to spending my days living in the present moment rather than the past, I allowed myself to turn my gaze toward the future. I imagined a large brick house set in the woods, with an entire back wall made of windows so that I could peer out toward the woods each morning to see deer walking by. I envisioned drinking cups of cocoa in front of a fireplace with my family around me and eating dinner in the dining room at a laughably oversized white and gold table. I dreamed of having a space in my home with a soft white carpet, flowered wallpaper, and meditation cushions where I could continue with my spiritual practice in a space that was entirely mine. I used all of my senses to bring this future reality to life within my mind, including the smells (sage and lavender), the sounds (birds and cicadas), and even the texture of the navy-blue velvet pieces of furniture with which I wanted to adorn each room. I made this dream so real in my mind that it would have been impossible for someone to tell me this wasn't my reality. It was as real to me as the small row home I was sitting in.

When I could see my desired potential reality with total clarity and no longer had shadow material blocking my ability to hold that vision, my external reality began to shift. The world shut down for a global pandemic, and my life as it had been couldn't continue. I had to give up my teaching position, switch all of my clients from in-person to virtual, and figure out how to manage a large caseload of psychotherapy clients while I had toddlers in the house and a husband working from home at the kitchen table. I was initially stressed and fearful, but I reminded myself that I had to let go and trust the Universe. I went back to my meditation pillow and began seeing visions of myself taking the small group program that I was currently running and scaling it in such a way that I could work fewer hours, make more money, and have a more powerful impact. Within a few months' time, my group shadow work program became my only work and my income more than quadrupled, all while the time I spent actually working dropped significantly.

Simultaneously, my husband had come to me suggesting that rather than buying a house, we should build one—in the woods. He had found a developer he liked who was building in a sizable patch of the forest in New Jersey, and with my new income, we could afford a much larger house than we had anticipated. When we saw the model home options from the developer, one design jumped off the page at me in a way that was startling. It was the Oxford Elite model, a home whose back wall consisted entirely of windows overlooking the forest, with a beautiful fireplace at the base to sit around with a family. The design also included five bedrooms and two offices, meaning that my Zen room was also about to become a reality.

I was shocked. It all came together almost too perfectly, as if the images in my mind were being presented to me on paper a mere few months later. It was as if someone had sketched what I had been daydreaming about. But that is exactly how reality can work—*if* we allow it to work with us.

Redefining Success

Think about the people you consider to be the most successful, the ones who seemingly have it all figured out. The archetypes in your mind might be celebrities, CEOs, or even family members whom everyone looks to as being the ones who have "made it." What you might notice is that the people in this group likely have quite a few things in common, like a strong work ethic, an abundance of opportunities, and a dash of luck. But the piece that I find the most fascinating about truly successful people is that they are constantly growing and evolving into newer, brighter, more aligned versions of themselves. It's as if they are consistently going through phases of metamorphosis and are always emerging even more radiant than they were just a few months before.

Life hack: we all have the capability to transform our lives based solely on the desire to do so.

Many of you who read that statement may have had some automatic thoughts pop into your mind, such as *yeah right, that's impossible,* or *easy for her to say.* If that was your inner monologue, that is a perfect example of the ego voice stepping in to keep you in the safety of the known state that you currently occupy. Remember that your growth is slightly threatening to the mind because it means your mind will have to create new neural pathways and subconscious feedback loops, and that would take a lot of effort to do. But constant growth and evolution are available to every single one of us when we realize how it is done and willingly choose to engage with it.

It all starts with understanding this very simple concept: *the version of you that you desire to be already exists.*

In physics, there is a principle called the quantum field, which is defined as an invisible energy field that exists outside of space and time. The quantum field is not made up of matter in the way that we typically understand it but instead is made of our perceived reality. We are taught to think chronologically, building on our yesterday to create our tomorrow. But those who are successful have learned that to create the life of your dreams, you need to build your tomorrow upon your desired future reality.

Let's begin by changing the way you think about time. Until now, you have likely thought of time as being linear, with events occurring in a chronological order along one long pathway. But I challenge you to see time as a series of potential realities, a number of paths all existing together in parallel, where you are able to choose whichever route you wish to walk on as you continue your journey. These pathways are present simultaneously; each one its own unique potential reality. But it's up to you which pathway you choose at any given moment.

Most of us walk a linear pathway, because we are building on what is behind us. The stereotypical American dream is the perfect example of this: graduate from high school, go on to college. Choose a steady career where you work from nine to five, and find a significant other along the way. Get married, purchase a home, and have two children soon after. This is the path that has been fed to us through movies, literature, society, and our families for the entirety of our lives.

This linear path doesn't allow for variations in the plan or opportunities for expansion because it is the path the brain determines as the known, which means it is considered the safest. It serves the subconscious feedback loop perfectly, as it keeps us in a state of homeostasis without much deviation from the norm and offers a solid plan back to homeostasis when we stray too far from the path. All with the end goal of creating a reality based on what the brain has already come to terms with and accepted as the only possible path forward.

When we follow this linear path, we are self-sabotaging our own success by blocking our ability for expansion. Growth comes from the unknown. It is crucial that you push through panic and grow from new experiences. And until you use the quantum field to hop onto new pathways and create new neural pathways and neuronal networks, you will remain as you have always been: stuck on your current linear path. And if you deviate from the path for any reason, whether it be purposeful or accidental, the body and mind go into a state of panic, sending you into anxiety, depression, or the feeling of needing to repress.

Become a Magnetic Manifester

According to quantum theory, every version of reality already exists. That means that your dreams are already a reality—you just need to draw them in to you. When you want to access the quantum realm to manifest a reality you desire, you have to remember this principle: we attract what we are, not what we want. That means that when we are attempting to manifest something into our lives, we must already have whatever it is that we want. Although this idea may sound counterintuitive, it rests on the notion that time isn't linear and every reality exists simultaneously. And we can use the help of our minds to access the quantum field.

Our brain creates our reality. Through a process called *mental rehearsal*, our mind uses its circuitry to connect neural pathways to conjure up images and emotions. And when these future realities are so real to the mind that it can't decipher the difference between real and imagined, it begins to seek out opportunities to allow that reality to be your new normal, thereby reinforcing what the brain now considers to be part of the known.

Here is an example of what it looks like when the brain uses mental rehearsal to create an alternate version of reality. Think back to the last time that you witnessed someone being physically hurt. Maybe it was one of your children or loved ones, or something you saw on television or in a movie. When you witnessed the way in which they were hurt, your neural pathways began to fire. The interesting thing to note here is that the way in which those pathways fire when we see someone else experiencing physical pain is like a muted version of what the person who is hurt is feeling. The same areas of the brain are activated, and if we were to scan both brains using an MRI, we would see the exact same areas of the brain lit up. The only difference between the two brains would be the intensity of the neurological reaction, with the person watching having a less intense response than the person experiencing it for themselves.

This phenomenon is the result of what are called *mirror neurons*, a phrase that describes the reaction in the brain when a bystander's neural pathways fire in precisely the same way as those of someone who is actively going through something. It is as if the brain itself, which is highly empathic, is using all of its sensory information to re-create a scenario so that it can fully understand the depths of what it is witnessing. Although the response is muted, it is still real. The bystander feels a small fraction of the pain the other person is feeling, as if it is happening to them too.

This is the same process that allows us to access future potential realities within the quantum field. If we know that our brains are highly empathic and able to create very real reactions within the mind and body based solely on understanding what something *might* feel like, we now know that we can use this process to our advantage to craft our desired reality using our thoughts.

Let's start with how to choose and create a potential reality. In order to quantum leap, you have to be able to access the new reality you desire on multiple sensory levels. You need to know what it looks like, feels like, sounds like, and so on. The more detailed the new reality, the more readily your mind, body, and spirit will accept this new potential as your future reality and help you access it. Including all of this sensory information activates chain reactions within the mind, causing neural pathways to fire as if this reality already existed. And once the mind, body, and spirit believe it already exists, you will intentionally take steps that will lead you to create this perfect life that already exists within the quantum.

Here's what this might look like. Let's say someone is working at a marketing firm and they are craving a change. This person is becoming tired of the monotony of the nine-to-five workday, and they feel a strong urge to get out of the place where they live. They also desire to work less than thirty hours a week but make more money than they do right now. This person wants to be able to travel the world and experience the beauty of nature and all it has to offer.

Knowing loosely what it is that they're yearning for, they decide to use the power of the quantum field to access their desired reality. They envision all the details of what this would look like, feeling completely what it is like for that potential reality to be their current reality. They continue holding the energy of this potential reality every day for two months.

What happens next is that they start making decisions about their life based on the new version of reality that they are living in energetically. This new version of them knows they need to use some of their paid leave from work to travel, and they decide to travel to Costa Rica. On the flight there, they hit it off with the person they are seated next to, and they tell this person all about their recent decision to grab for this aligned version of reality. When the flight ends, the person seated next to them hands over their business card and says they should talk more. They find out that this person isn't just anyone, but is the head of a marketing firm that wants hire a new team lead. The job would include a lot of travel to beautiful locations, but the hours worked would be incredibly flexible.

In this hypothetical situation, each decision this person made was based on their living in their future reality to such an extent that opportunities began to show up for them. For instance, if they continued believing they were stuck at their job, they never would have chosen to take time off. And if they hadn't been feeling this strong need to travel and be in nature, they never would have booked their trip to Costa Rica. If they were feeling bogged down by work and the state their life was in, they wouldn't have caught the attention of the marketing executive who was now hiring them for their dream job.

Imagine quantum leaping as co-creating with the Universe, with you and the Universe working in tandem to make your thoughts a reality. If you are negative, the Universe reinforces that. If you expect opportunities to show up, the Universe brings them to you. If you are open to creating change, the Universe provides challenges for you to move through so that change can occur. The relationship between human beings and the Universe is one of total reciprocity, and you can use that to co-create any reality that you seek, no matter how outrageous it may seem.

Here's an exercise you can use to begin the work of tapping into alternate potential realities from the quantum field.

The Perfect World

This is an old therapy exercise, one that I've added a twist to that's based on the work of Dr. Joe Dispenza. It's excellent for manifestation because it will help us get extremely clear about what you are calling in.

Start by getting a pen and your journal and writing out a specific manifestation you are working toward at the top. Examples are "Career," "Relationship," and "Home."

MEDITATION

Close your eyes. Allow everything you brought with you to the meditation—mentally, physically, or emotionally—to wash away into pure white light. See the white light all around you and imagine yourself waking up in the future in a perfect world. This world is perfect because whatever you are attempting to manifest (the career, the relationship, the home, and so on) has been realized, and your life is now wildly different. Having woken up, what do you notice? Where are you? Is it the home you currently occupy or a new one? What does it look like? How do you know your manifestation has come to pass?

Continue allowing yourself to indulge this fantasy fully and completely until you are so familiar with the details that you know you won't forget them.

When you finish your meditation, write the numbers 1 to 5 underneath the title (whatever you chose to manifest), and list the details of what your manifestation will look like based on what you saw during your meditation.

Underneath that, write the numbers 1 to 5 again, and list the details of what you know achieving that manifestation to feel like. I suggest including gratitude, because gratitude is an emotion that is retrospective—that means the brain will believe your manifestation has already happened.

Below that, list any other additional sensory details you want to include (like the way it will smell, sound, taste, and so on) to add depth to your vision.

Here's an example list:

HOME
What does it look like?
1. Five-bedroom home
2. Located near the ocean
3. Tons of natural light
4. Balcony
5. Large windows

How does it feel?
1. Gratitude
2. Peace
3. Elation
4. Bliss
5. Excitement

What other sensory information is present?
1. I can hear the waves from my house.
2. I can smell the salty air.

If this were your list, you might imagine yourself waking up in a cozy bedroom with a soft white comforter nestled around you. You stretch out your body as the sunlight hits your face from your large bedroom windows, and you feel immense gratitude for this morning. You fold back the comforter and step off the bed onto a lush shag rug. You walk to your designer kitchen, noticing the intricate patterns on the marble countertops and the stunning gold hardware on the white cabinets. You make a cup of coffee with your French press, inhaling the aroma of the rich coffee as it brews. When your coffee is ready, you pour it into your favorite mug and walk out onto your ocean-view balcony, sipping away at the steaming drink while you watch the waves crash on the beach. You take a seat in your cozy chair and inhale deeply. You can smell the salty air, and you can feel the sun warming your skin and the light breeze at it passes over you. Inside, you feel a deep sense of gratitude for this life that you have created here. When you walk back into the house, you notice the abundant number of large windows that allow the sunlight to find its way into the home. You feel at home, at peace, and that this is exactly where you are meant to be.

When I was unknowingly manifesting my dream home, I used this exact process to align myself with the pathway that would get me to my desired future reality. And in a short amount of time, I was standing inside of the home of my dreams, chills rushing down my spine, knowing that I had made this happen by retrieving this potential reality from within the quantum realm.

Accessing a new potential reality is relatively easy when you follow this process. It can range from something as small as calling in a promotion at work, to something as large as manifesting a new career altogether. Once you have chosen what you want to manifest and practice this exercise, continue recalling your perfect world on a daily basis. Take ten minutes out of your day and allow yourself to revisit it, making the details concrete within your mind. The brain, after revisiting this place consistently, will begin to mistake this future potential for your current reality, and it will alter your subconscious feedback loop and neural pathways to match this information. That means that the brain will seek experiences that reinforce this new reality, allowing you to find and take part in opportunities that align you more closely with this reality, ones you might not have found if you hadn't begun using this tool. Do this until your manifestation has come to pass.

6

Learn to Listen

During the fall of 2021, a lot of things were shifting for me personally. I was actively working on accessing new pathways within the quantum field to see just how far I could push myself to reach. Because so much was moving within my world, I wanted to ensure that I was on the right track. My personal go-to exercise for this is to ask my spirit guides if I am headed in the right direction, asking them to give me a very specific sign. I connected with them through a short meditation, and I asked out loud, "Guides, if I am on the right path in my career, please show me owls today."

I hosted a group call with the women of my shadow work program late one morning, and as all of the women hopped on Zoom, I couldn't help but notice that one of my students was sitting in a different room from where she normally did for our calls. Behind her was a quilt with designs of owls every few inches across the entirety of it. I made a comment about it to her, and she mentioned that she had just felt called to sit in that room instead for our session, though she wasn't sure why. That was my first sign, confirmation that I was on the right path.

That afternoon, my children returned home from school excited to show me their art projects that they had completed in class. My daughter had made three bookmarks, one of which was an owl. She handed me that one and told me, "The owl bookmark is for you!" Sign received. My son opened up his folder and showed me a children's magazine everyone in his class had received that day. On the cover? A beautiful photograph of a barn owl, its white face and honey-brown feathers catching me by surprise. Another sign received.

Now, even I was a bit skeptical after receiving so many owls that day. Maybe I was off base and it was because we were in the northeastern part of the country during fall. *Owls must be common here this time of year*, I thought. I decided to test this confirmation a bit further two weeks later, when I went to Florida for a festival with my husband. I woke up on the first morning of the festival in seventy-degree Florida sunshine, and I asked my guides again to show me an owl today if my career was on the right track.

A few hours later, we arrived at the festival to discover that the theme for this year was Zen (one that I found perfectly fitting for the intention I had set for this trip). After entering at the main gates and moving onto a large, lush grass field, we began scoping out the area to see where we wanted to go first. We decided to make our way into the VIP area to get something to eat before beginning to explore the space. We rounded the corner to find the line to enter and allowed security guards to check our wristbands so we could go into the gated zone. Once inside, we were face to face with a gigantic wooden owl—a prop for influencers to take photographs with at the festival for social media. I couldn't believe it. I pointed it out to my husband and told him of my request to my spirit guides, to which he said, "Danielle, look around! There's owls everywhere in here." I let my eyes scan the area and noticed that the barricades all had the faces of owls on them. Hundreds of owls were staring back at me. This was beyond my wildest dreams.

But it became even wilder when we finally made our way to the main stage, which had a beautiful, intricate design of—you guessed it—an owl, complete with blinking eyes and a turning head. That night, as fireworks burst over the main stage, a drone light show began overhead, the finale of which was all of the drones turning into a gigantic owl flying over the stage, to the amazement of the crowd.

Typically, when I ask for signs from my guides, they aren't quite this prominent. But when I closed my eyes and checked in with my guides, they told me that for the first time in my life, I was exactly where I needed to be.

Cosmic Breadcrumbs

Everything happens for a reason. Every heartbreak, betrayal, loss, and seemingly hopeless situation was designed by the universe to move you in one direction or another. This is often easier to see in hindsight than it is while you're in the thick of it. So often during shadow work, I'll have clients who recount the lowest moments of their lives with extreme gratitude, noting that those low moments led them to unimaginable highs, and sometimes even toward their soul's purpose.

When the universe wants you to alter your current course, it will often attempt to gently lead you down a new path. I call these paths *cosmic breadcrumbs* because of the trail that is being laid out before your feet. When you become skilled at following these cosmic bread-crumbs, life becomes exceedingly simple because your movements, behaviors, and choices are all divinely led. That's not to say that life will be sunshine and roses one hundred percent of the time. There may still be some difficult moments (life is life after all, and we're here to have a full human experience). But when you're following the cosmic breadcrumbs, you'll find that you're less at war with yourself and more at peace with your life because you have a deeper understanding and profound connection to the Universe as it guides you down paths that feel completely aligned.

The opposite is true when you're not listening to the signs you're being given. Before being diagnosed with cancer, I had years of signs pointing me toward slowing down and resting. As I ignored the cosmic breadcrumbs, the messages became much louder and more intense, including a particularly painful bout of shingles when I was only twenty-one years old, an illness that typically doesn't show up in young people unless they are suffering from severe chronic stress. I ignored the signs that I was receiving until I received my cancer diagnosis, when the Universe gave me no option but to change paths away from my course.

The universe is often trying to communicate with us to help us heal from our shadow before our shadow becomes all-encompassing. If we can act early, our unconscious memories are not given the opportunity to create disorder within our minds, bodies, and energy. But when we ignore the cosmic breadcrumbs we are being given, the information that is stuck in the shadow can wreak havoc on us as the shadow information grows beyond capacity and spills out into our subconscious and conscious awareness. Not to mention that when we are able to follow the path the Universe is working to put us on through shadow work and healing, our lives become infinitely easier. This is why listening to nudges from the universe is an important part of any spiritual journey.

Cosmic breadcrumbs can look like a variety of things, ranging from number sequences or repetitions (such as 11:11 or 222), to opportunities that continually present themselves (such as being offered speaking gigs from multiple separate sources), to hearing the same song on the radio every time you start your car. Begin noticing the cosmic breadcrumbs and see if you can tell what was happening right before you received a sign from the Universe. Whatever came before the cosmic breadcrumb can help you ascertain what it is that the Universe is encouraging you to pursue. Allow the cosmic breadcrumbs to be confirmation or validation that you are on the right path.

What Are Spirit Guides?

Spirit guides are spirits that are found in another plane of existence that are here to help you along your journey. I refer to the space that they occupy as *the upper realm*, but you can choose to refer to it however you would like. When I access the upper realm, the imagery that I see within my mind's eye consists of luscious, fluffy clouds that you can walk on and beautiful, deep blues, pale pinks, and shades of lavender. When I'm transported there, everything feels light, as if the emotional baggage that I carry around my shoulders in the human realm is wiped away in an instant. When people speak about Heaven, this is where I believe they go. And the upper realm is where it is easiest to connect to many of the spirit guides that you can work with.

Some guides have been with you throughout your entire life (or even lifetimes), while others come during specific moments to help you through your current experiences. Spirit guides can consist of loved ones who have passed on, angels, spirit animals, ascended masters, galactic groups, and ancestors. Developing a strong relationship with your guides can help you tremendously throughout your spiritual journey, as they can act like a light in a tunnel, showing you where to move next or what to avoid on your path.

Many people miss the signs their spirit guides are giving them because they aren't paying attention to the present moment. They may be too singularly focused on what they are doing next, or maybe they are ruminating on troubles from their past. Either way, they are missing the signs that are right in front of them by not being in the here and now. When doing shadow work, it is important to have a strong connection to your guides, so that they can help you stay on the right path, rather than getting wrapped up in the darkness and swept away by it.

I like to advise my students that connecting with spirit guides is a two-way street. If you want them to give you signs, you have to be willing to connect with them as well. You must get used to speaking to them on a regular basis, often simply telling them about yourself as a way of showing your openness to the connection. Doing this will open the door to the relationship between you and your guides. And when you begin to work your end of the relationship, they will begin to work their end of the relationship as well.

Opening the Door: A Meditation to Connect with Spirit Guides

Begin by sitting or lying in a comfortable position. Start taking deep breaths, breathing in through the nose and out through the mouth. Place your hands on your stomach and focus on making your belly expand and contract with each breath. As you allow this breath to fill your body, imagine yourself opening up at the crown of your head, allowing a beam of light to ascend out of your crown toward the heavens. Feel that beam of light growing stronger and visualize its color as you connect, noticing any physical sensations you might be experiencing at the crown. Once that connection feels strong, begin speaking to your guides (out loud is best, but in your mind is fine as well).

The first time you do this meditation, begin by talking to them and letting them know about you. Fill them in on the details of your life, the way you would with a new friend. This step will help establish that the door is open. End by thanking them for connecting with you.

The second time you do this meditation, ask your spirit guides to show you a specific sign so that you know they are communicating with you. Here is a list of signs you can ask for, but please feel free to choose anything you would like:

● Feathers
● Dimes

- Repeating number (11:11, 222, 333, and so on)
- Specific animals
- Ladybugs

End the meditation by thanking them in advance for the signs you will receive.

As your connection to your spirit guides grows stronger with the repetition of this meditation, you may begin to see or hear your guides. If you do, don't be afraid—this is completely normal, and it just means that your connection is getting stronger. Begin by speaking to the guides directly, and allow yourself to receive the guidance you seek. Always end each meditation with gratitude for this guidance.

As you practice this exercise continually, connecting with your spirit guides will become exponentially easier. Eventually, you may even begin to notice that your guides have distinct voices, share certain types of imagery, or affect your physical body in various ways. When that begins to happen, you can begin to decipher who's who on your spirit guide team.

Types of Spirit Guides

LOVED ONES WHO HAVE PASSED

After we exit this physical plane through death, our souls linger before reincarnating again. Some souls reincarnate quite soon, and others may wait hundreds of years before returning to a physical body. One of the factors influencing whether someone chooses to linger is if they choose to work as a spirit guide for a time, guiding people on the Earth plane whom they cared for in life.

Deceased loved ones act much the way they did when they were alive, but are subject to fewer of the highs and lows of human emotion. If you lost a grandmother who was insistent that you settle down and get married, she may continue to nudge you along that same path, helping you to accomplish this from the afterlife by sending potential partners to you. Or if you had an uncle who acted as a mentor in your career, it is possible that he will continue to bolster your career after he has left this plane by helping push opportunities your way.

ANGELS

Angels are beings that exist beyond our comprehension. They live not as you and I do in physical bodies, but as pure loving energy. Angels help bring us back into alignment with the universe, guiding us back toward love, light, and inner peace. There are many angels and archangels, each with its own unique mission and purpose, and although many religions speak of angels, they are nondenominational presences here to shift humanity as a whole. To connect with angels, all we need do is ask. They are always ready to step in and guide us along our journey if we are willing to bring them into the fold.

SPIRIT ANIMALS

Spirit animals (also referred to as familiars) are animal guides that have distinct messages to share with you on your spiritual journey. The natural connection that animals have to Mama Gaia (i.e., the Earth) and all her ancient wisdom makes them the perfect guides to bring us back into alignment with her. They are often a reminder for us to slow down, connect with our roots, and find our way back toward nature. When you connect with an animal during meditation, slow down and listen to what they are bringing your attention toward.

Every animal has its own symbology, but I would recommend that you try to connect with spirit animals yourself to ask them what they are trying to show you. For example, an Internet search on the symbology of a blackbird might steer you in the wrong direction if you believe they are a bad omen, but if you listen to what the bird is trying to convey, you might find that they are actually there to guide you toward a major transformation.

ASCENDED MASTERS

Ascended masters are high-vibrational beings that were once in human form, as you and I are now. These beings have achieved their soul's purpose in the physical realm and now exist to help usher others toward self-discovery and enlightenment. Every ascended master has had thousands of lifetimes in a physical form, where their soul continued to learn everything that it could while in the physical plane. They moved through their karma, integrated their shadow, and learned to become the master of the limitations of their humanity, thereby reaching true enlightenment.

Ascended masters are particularly helpful as spirit guides when you need help navigating karmic situations.

Because they once existed in human form, they have a unique understanding of how to help move you through karmic loops with grace and compassion. Call upon your ascended masters when you feel like you are continually facing the same problem repeatedly and can find no solution for how to move through it.

GALACTIC GROUPS

Here is a number that may blow your mind: Scientists estimate that there are hundreds of billions of galaxies in existence. The Milky Way galaxy is only one of these. It's beyond comprehension to imagine that the vastness of our solar system as we know it is a mere pinprick in the spectrum of galactic life. Given that we still know so little about the infinite nature of existence, it's no surprise to find out that our souls predate our time on Earth and are much older than you may realize. And just as there are ascended masters that were once human, we also have ascended masters from our previous incarnations in the cosmos that were once living, breathing beings. These are our galactic groups, a unique form of spirit guides that are here to help us align with the love of the universe. These galactic groups connect with us wherever and whenever our souls incarnate to help guide us on our journeys.

The galactic groups that we connect with are most often ones that hail from the same planetary groups that our souls do, such as (but not limited to) the Pleiadians, Arcturians, Sirians, and Andromedans. No matter which galactic group you connect with, they all share the Universal message of love, light, and joy.

Working with them will often mean being guided down a path of connecting with the stars and finding ways to uplift humanity.

ANCESTORS

Your ancestors differ from your loved ones who have passed because they are from further up your bloodline, many generations before you were born. These ancestors have chosen to remain as spirit guides rather than reincarnating so that they can assist you in remembering your roots and the traditions of your family; they act to guide you back to who you are at your core. Your ancestors may seek to help you break generational curses and karmic loops that exist within your bloodline, and they are the perfect guides to work with during the process of ancestral healing. They can also help you access gifts from your bloodline, old magic and wisdom that was present in your family that has been passed down to you for when you were ready to learn and embody it.

You can also connect with your ancestors from your soul's past incarnations (your galactic group would be an example of this). I have had a past life as a Native American woman from the Lenape tribe, and connecting with my ancestors from that lifetime opened up a multitude of new opportunities for my healing and growth. For instance, my Lenape guides have taught me how to use the earth to heal, and they have also led me to build my home on Lenape lands so that I can connect with the earth in the same place where my soul has done so once before. They have also urged me to read about the horrific tragedies that the Native American people of this region experienced, to remember what has happened so that I may help end karmic loops connected to these devastating events.

Learn to Connect

Something that I often see in those who consider themselves new to spirituality is a heavy dependence on other people to interpret signs from spirit guides. Although having a mentor is a helpful experience, it is not a necessary one here and can even block your ability to connect with your guides. In truth, our spirit guides connect with all of us differently based on the ways in which we are willing to receive messages from them. That means that 11:11 will mean something very different to me than if a spirit guide sends the same number sequence to you. It is imperative that you allow yourself to trust your intuition as you navigate the early stages of connecting to your guides. The more you rely on your own inner knowing, the quicker and more effective your correspondence will be. You'll also learn to trust yourself as you move through your journey on to more complicated tasks such as shadow work. Trust yourself. Imagine that there is no way that you can be wrong. And listen to your gut above all else.

If you need further confirmation of your own inner wisdom, allow yourself to use the human pendulum technique described earlier in this book. Doing so will help confirm what you already know to be true, and this will reinforce your belief in yourself and your own abilities.

The Four Clairs

Although some might believe that we need to rely on spiritually gifted individuals to access information from other realms, the truth is that every person on this planet has divine spiritual gifts. We are all born with an innate ability to tap into psychic wisdom, though those gifts may manifest differently within each of us. In spiritual communities, these gifts are referred to as the *four clairs*. They are clairvoyance (inner seeing), clairaudience (inner hearing), clairsentience (inner feeling), and claircognizance (inner knowing). Depending on our soul's personal journey, some of these gifts may be more developed than others. But we still have access to all of them, along with the ability to strengthen each one until all four are potent and strong.

Clairvoyance

The gift of sight is typically the spiritual gift we most often associate with divine abilities. This may be because of media influence, such as movies like *The Sixth Sense*, in which a child sees ghosts, or books like

Charlie Saint Cloud, in which a young man has the ability to see those who have crossed over. But contrary to popular belief, clairvoyance is not synonymous with psychic abilities, and many people who consider themselves psychic rely on all four of the clairs to interpret messages from spirit or would consider their other clairs to be stronger.

Clairvoyance can look different to different people. Certainly, sometimes it is the ability for people to see spirits with the naked eye. But often it is subtler, such as seeing spirits in your mind's eye or seeing flashes of images that are meant to be metaphorical. For instance, having a vision in your mind's eye of someone chained to the earth might mean that person feels stuck in their current situation. Clairvoyance can also be seeing auras around people, either with the naked eye or with your mind's eye. This might look like staring at someone and seeing a faint outline of a specific color hovering around them, like a deep blue, or a mix of light yellow and green swirling together.

Clairvoyance can be strengthened through practice (as can all the clairs). Choosing to strengthen your clairvoyance can help you more readily interpret messages from spirit and help you gain clarity as you navigate through your journey. Asking yourself to conjure up detailed images in your mind, and then imagining them changing, can be a helpful exercise to boost your clairvoyance. You can use the following details to begin this practice.

Strengthen Your Clairvoyance

Begin by looking at this image of the moon for thirty seconds:

After studying this picture, close your eyes and attempt to recall as many details from the image as you can. Repeat this process until you can see the moon in perfect detail.

Once you can solidly recall the image of the moon in your mind's eye, it is time to kick it up a notch. I want you to imagine the moon shifting shape until it becomes a full moon. Imagine the stars around the moon twinkling as time passes. Allow yourself to alter it in your mind. Continue to practice until you can easily manipulate the image in whatever ways you imagine. The more you do this, the stronger your visual abilities will become.

After you have been strengthening your clairvoyance for a time, or if you are naturally inclined toward this gift, you may notice visual images popping into your head in a seemingly random way. During conversations, you might see an image of two people playing tug-of-war, potentially indicating that the person that you are speaking with is in the middle of some sort of back-and-forth with another person. You might even see images in your mind's eye of loved ones who have crossed over, indicating that they are there with you. Continue working on your clairvoyance to help aid your spiritual journey, especially as this gift can be helpful during shadow work.

Clairaudience

Clairaudience is the ability to hear messages from spirit in your mind. Many people talk to themselves throughout the day via an inner monologue; clairaudience is different in that it often sounds like calm, even-toned messages. There typically isn't strong emotion behind them, and the messages received can be quite short or even clichéd. As with clairvoyance, there are two ways that someone with this gift might receive it: with their ears, or in their mind.

People who are clairaudient often don't recognize that they have this gift. Clairaudience can manifest as ringing in the ears, because the frequency that messages from other realms come to us on are much higher in pitch than what we typically hear. Those with strong clairaudience may find that when they daydream, they can clearly hear the noises of the place where they are imagining themselves, such as waves crashing on a beach. Individuals with clairaudience can also sometimes hear the noises spirits make, such as soft footsteps, or doors creaking. In fact, this gift can sometimes unnerve people when they realize that it is spirit that they are hearing, and the resulting fear can block their ability to receive clairaudient messages that might be helpful for them on their journey.

Those who have naturally strong clairaudience are often gifted musicians or linguists because their ears are attuned to subtleties that the average person's ears would not pick up on. But even if clairaudience is not a gift you feel you have naturally, you can work to increase your clairaudience with simple exercises.

Strengthen Your Clairaudience

Choose any song and listen to it for thirty seconds. Then shut off the music and try to re-create those thirty seconds of sound in your mind. Can you hear the notes, the words, the background noise, or the individual instruments?

Continue this practice until you feel you have adequately re-created the music in your mind with near perfect detail.

Stretch your abilities even further by imagining the next thirty seconds. Choose what they will sound like, and allow the first thirty seconds to flow seamlessly into the continuation you have created. Continue this practice until you have composed a beautiful, unified sound experience in your mind.

Clairsentience

When people are not yet fully tapped into the spiritual realm, I find that they identify most with the gift of clairsentience. Clairsentience is clear feeling, and it is the gift of being able to tap into emotions within and around oneself. Those who are clairsentient frequently refer to themselves as being empaths because they can feel, and are often influenced by, the emotions of those around them.

Think for a moment about how it feels to be next to someone who has a major depressive disorder. You might feel that the air gets a bit denser and heavier. You may even feel that heaviness within your own body while you are in their presence. You could become sluggish and lethargic, maybe craving stimulants to help bring you back to your normal energetic state.

Now imagine being with someone who is manic. Their intense energy levels might have an opposite effect, making you experience some anxiety as your own energy level escalates. You might feel chaotic, or as if you need some space to calm yourself down and come back to your normal energy level.

If you resonate with either of those experiences, you might be clairsentient. But there's more to it than just being able to feel the energy of those around you.

Another way people with clairsentience might experience their gift is to have a physical reaction when they're on the right track. When spirit gives you a message, they might accompany it with chills down one arm or the feeling of tapping on your leg. When working with clients, that is often how I know that whatever message I just gave them is what they really needed to hear in that moment.

Clairsentience is often the first gift people identify with, but it can still be strengthened and fine-tuned. Use the following exercise to increase your clairsentience.

Claircognizance

The psychic gift of claircognizance is one's ability to "just know" things. Claircognizance is when you suddenly have an immediate answer to a question, as if the answer simply appeared within your mind. In the spiritual community, this instantaneous retrieval of information is known as a download, and it can be thought of as being akin to a download on a computer. The one variation is that a psychic download is immediate, whereas a computer download may take some time to complete.

When claircognizant people receive a download, it can be about absolutely anything, from an ailment that another person might be suffering from to an answer to an existential question that they might have about their life, such as why they repeatedly choose significant others who take advantage of them.

Signs that you might have the gift of claircognizance range from being the person many turn to for advice (I knew a lot of psychotherapists with this gift while I was still practicing) or having "aha moments" for yourself and others that lead you or them down the right path. Another example could be knowing when someone is going to pass away before it occurs. It can be slightly tricky to discern whether you are having spontaneous thoughts or true claircognizant downloads. One way to differentiate the two is to think about downloads as "lightbulb moments" versus something more circular. If a thought appears and disappears quite rapidly, that is a download. If it's something you are mulling over for an extended period, that is a thought.

Strengthen Your Claircognizance

Use the Four Seasons Test to help you develop strong claircognizant abilities.

PREPARATION:

Take a piece of paper and cut it evenly into four quadrants.

On each quadrant, write the name of one of the four seasons: spring, summer, autumn, or winter.

Fold each individual piece up so that you can no longer see what is written on the paper. Try to fold each paper in the same way so that you cannot discern which is which.

THE TEST:

Shuffle the four pieces of paper in a hat or a bowl. Reach in and grab one piece of paper. As you hold it in your hand, trust yourself to intuitively know which season is written on the paper you're holding. Unfold the paper to see whether you are correct.

This is a skill that may take some time to develop, so try not to be frustrated if you guess wrong in the beginning. Over time and with ample practice, your claircognizance will grow exponentially until you intuitively know which season is written on your paper every time you attempt this.

Let Go of Fear

Now that you know how to strengthen your intuitive abilities and connect with your guides, we have to discuss the most common block to our gifts that exists within all people. The block is fear, and it clogs up your channel (psychic pathway), halting your ability to receive divine guidance.

We are not born afraid of our spiritual gifts. Although fear is one of the few emotions that we have at birth (and technically speaking, fear develops even sooner than that, as it is present when you are still within the womb), a fear of our innate psychic abilities and connection to spirit is something that we are conditioned to feel over time. It is extremely common for children to have imaginary friends (spirit guides that they can see), recall their past lives, hear things from the upper realm, and interact with people who have crossed over. But as children share these experiences with the adults in their lives, they are very often made to feel afraid or ashamed of their abilities. The negative reaction of the adults in their life undoubtedly creates a subconscious feedback loop around psychic abilities and spiritual connection being something to fear, so their mind and body work together to shut down these gifts. The memory of these connections ends up being stored in the unconscious, sometimes never to be seen again.

This fear is reinforced by outside sources in an effort to control the masses and stop them from being able to access their own internal wisdom. These sources include media and religion, two external sources that are used to control people on a grand scale. When we think about connecting with spirit, it often makes us recall scary movies in which spirits use human bodies as hosts, or to hurt them on their human plane. Although this is factually incorrect, it makes for excellent ticket sales, as movie producers continue to up the ante and capitalize on fear. Think about how your body reacts in the theater when a grotesque-looking spirit pops up behind someone, with the undertone being that the spirit came with the intention to harm the person. When you see this propaganda enough times, it's easy to believe that encounters with other realms are bound to be harmful and dangerous. And that is enough to make anyone pause before connecting with their internal guidance system.

Religion is another arena where connection to spirit is often manipulated and warped. In some religious contexts, only certain people are allowed to interact with, and act on behalf of, the spirit. These chosen people have to devote themselves to that particular faith, and so-called laypeople need to use these chosen ones to communicate with spirit guides, as they themselves aren't worthy. Furthermore, when laypeople do tap into their innate psychic abilities, they are often deemed crazy, and historically they've been persecuted for this connection, which is sometimes labeled demonic.

When we shy away from our abilities out of fear, we are giving our power away. In those moments, we are allowing other people to tell us what is best for us and for our lives. In truth, we all carry within ourselves at all times the answers for who we are, what we need, and how to live. We are our own inner guru, and we absolutely need to learn to let go of our fear of that fact.

Fear carries a very dense vibration. And when people learn to be afraid, they are altering their own energetic structure to match that vibration. Remaining at that lower frequency is like turning the dial on your radio to a space between channels where there is only static—no clear, concise messages. It's only when we learn to release fear and learn to love our gifts that we can change our frequency to match that of the loving energy of divine realms, allowing us to easily access and use help from our spirit guides and our intuition. And once you can do that, the radio messages are clear, vibrant, and loud!

Here are some truths to understand about spiritual connection to help you remove that fear you may be connected to:

1. You have spiritual abilities; everyone does. You just might not realize what they are or how to manifest them.

2. Children are not afraid of this connection because they are not born afraid of it. They happily interact with spirit until some other outside force interrupts the connection, whether it be caregivers, media, religion, or another external source.

3. Depending on how spirit connects with you, it can be a bit scary at first, but only because it will kickstart the subconscious feedback loop of fear that is already firmly embedded into your mind and body. Challenge it by remaining open and unafraid.

Remind yourself of these points as you strengthen your clairs, and trust that you are exactly where you need to be. As your connection to yourself grows and your fear dissipates, your abilities will strengthen exponentially, allowing you to tap into your inner wisdom effortlessly. And when you become your own inner guru, trusting yourself to move into your shadow and rewire your mind, body, and spirit will be effortless as well.

Fear may present itself during shadow work, because the nature of shadow work is to go back to moments that have been frightening for you in the past so that you can heal them completely. But healing these moments means setting yourself free as the emotional and energetic weight of them no longer clings to you. You may also be afraid of finding that you have a lot of darkness within you that your psyche has been attempting to repress. But darkness within is a normal part of human life! We all have aspects of ourselves that we've attempted to push away and hide. Shadow work is an invitation to engage all aspects of who you are and to integrate them fully, trusting that this process will create ease within your mind, body, and energy and allow you to feel more healed than you may have believed possible.

I've been asked many times how I can do something as heavy as shadow work or if I'm afraid of it. And my answer is always the same: I'm not afraid of my darkness. I'm inspired by it. Because within the darkest corners of my soul, I found myself.

7

Back to the Past

About a year into my regular shadow work practice, I stumbled across a past life I hadn't yet seen. I saw myself as a very young girl, about five or six years old, with long, chestnut-colored hair and fair skin. I was living with my parents in a quaint house in New England during the colonial period, which was evidenced by the clothing and architecture. I was sitting near a fire feeling its luscious warmth on my cold skin, and my mother was singing softly to herself as she worked behind me. I could smell the food she was preparing, and I felt the comfort of her presence deep within my heart. I could tell that in this lifetime, my mother meant the world to me.

Within a few moments of my soul's arrival to this time, an eerie feeling washed over my body. I began to feel anxious with anticipation, as something that I was unsure of was about to unfold. My mother and I began to hear men's voices outside of our home, the volume continually increasing until there was a very loud knock at the door. My mother, a slim woman with wavy, dark brown hair, a cream-colored apron, and a worried look on her face that exaggerated her age, reluctantly answered the door. Because I was reexperiencing this life as a young child, the memory felt less clear cognitively than others I had experienced in the past, though the visuals were vibrant. I was see-ing this memory through the lens of a child, less sure of myself and what I was seeing than I would have been had I been an adult at that time. As a child, I had to rely heavily on the emotions that I felt to decipher what I was experiencing. And what I felt at this moment was sheer terror.

A large man, possibly the leader of this group, back-handed my mother across the face with such force that it knocked her to the floor. I let out a terrified scream as my mother urged me to run away and hide. I felt frozen to the spot as two more men entered our home and hoisted my mother up. She struggled to get away, and I watched as her face, contorted in pain and with blood trickling down from the corner of her mouth, as she pleaded to be released. "Please don't hurt my daughter," she repeated over and over, as the men who had seized her took her out of the home. The men paid me no mind, and when they left, I ran to the door to watch them carry my world away from me. When I attempted to run after her, my father came in from out-side and pulled my tiny, wailing body into his arms to hold me back. He whispered into my ear that we were safe now, that he had protected us. My body was flooded with adrenaline and cortisol, every cell in my body begging me to run, to fight, to do *something* to get my mother back.

When we visit past lives, time collapses in on itself, and that was true of this past life experience. Because the next scene I dropped into was one in which my mother, still wearing the same clothes, though they were torn and filthy, had a noose around her neck in a town square. She was standing with a few other women, all of whom looked beaten down and dirty from obvious mistreatment while awaiting this public execution. As I looked around the square, it was clear to me that the whole town was present to watch; this was a morbid spectacle that was to be enjoyed collectively by all of the townspeople. My father held my hand as my mother's life ended, and I hated him for it.

After coming back into a state of full consciousness, I journaled about the experience (a practice I highly recommend for anyone diving into shadow work). Here is what I gathered:

1. My mother was accused of witchcraft during the time of an outbreak of hysteria in colonial New England.
2. My father had a hand in delivering my mother to the hysterical townspeople for her trial and execution.
3. My father believed he was protecting me, but in truth he was protecting himself.

4. I was powerless in this situation. Having no voice to defend my mother because of my age led to a marked power imbalance between my father and me.

Here is where the story gets interesting. I recognized the souls of my parents in that past life as my current father (who was my father in that lifetime) and his mother, my paternal grandmother (who was my mother in that lifetime). More on this later. First, I want to help you begin connecting with your own past lives.

Connecting with Your Past Lives

Our past lives hold rich information about where our soul has been and what our soul's purpose is. To begin your past life journey, answer the following questions:

1. What subjects were you most drawn to in history class?

When your classmates were falling asleep but your interest was piqued, there was a reason. We are more likely to be interested in and engaged with subjects we have a direct connection to. If you were highly invested in learning about ancient Egypt or about the Tudor dynasty in England, it is likely that it's because you were alive during those time periods and connected to them in some way.

2. What historical books, television shows, and movies are you interested in watching?

For the same reasons as with the previous answer, the media you consume may be a window into your past. Taking in certain media may give you nostalgia and a longing for a home you don't remember because it is from a previous life.

3. What cultures are you connected to that you are not a blood descendant of?

If you have a deep reverence for a specific culture, especially if you have no direct connection to it in this life, that is an indicator that you have had a past life there. For instance, if you feel strongly connected to ancient China and find yourself wanting to acquire ancient Chinese paintings, jewelry, or artifacts, this is a sign of a past life there. You may also find that items from this culture find their way to you in the form of gifts from others, a nudge from a spirit guide to pay attention to what you have received.

◒

Once you have these answers, try connecting all the dots that have appeared throughout your life and that suggest how these places have been connected to you. Here is an example of what this might look like:

After answering all of the questions, I can see with clarity that I've always had a strong connection to ancient Egypt. Something about it has always felt like home, and I'm drawn to it in a way that's disproportionate to what one might expect.

When you have been able to identify a few potential past lives, you can choose to use shadow work to access memories of them by setting specific intentions to see those particular lives.

You already know that you have had multiple past lives, but what you might be missing is the reason your soul chooses to reincarnate over and over. In fact, when I tell people that their soul has had hundreds or even thousands of lifetimes, the first question I typically get is "why?" This is my answer:

Our souls reincarnate for a simple purpose: to learn lessons.
This allows our souls to continually grow and expand.

When our souls show up in a new lifetime, they come with the purpose of building on the lessons they learned in prior lifetimes, causing more growth and expansion to occur. They choose to have heartbreaks, immeasurable grief, and pain beyond imagining, all to fulfill this purpose—because when we hit rock bottom, our souls are given opportunities to make choices that align with the highest version of themselves, thus fulfilling their true purpose.

Our souls incarnate in what I like to refer to as *soul pods*, meaning we repeat lives with souls that we have already experienced other lifetimes with. Your parents, siblings, significant others, children, extended family, co-workers, and close friends have likely had lifetimes with you before this one. And whatever struggles you encountered in those previous lifetimes with them will seek to be resolved in this one or in future lifetimes. This phenomenon is called a *karmic loop*.

In this newly discovered past life that I experienced with my father and grandmother, all three of us had karmic loops that needed to be healed in this current lifetime. Let's break them down by relationship:

My father and grandmother: In that past life, my father sacrificed his wife, which was a massive betrayal of trust. To heal that breach in this lifetime, the two of them needed to build trust from the ground up and learn from that past mistake. Doing so would have healed that karmic loop. Unfortunately, because of an early trauma in my father's life caused by the negligence of my grandmother, this karmic loop was reinforced instead of resolved.

My father and I: In that past life, I felt powerless because of my inability to use my voice to defend my mother, and I transferred that sadness into an extreme hatred for my father, the man I deemed responsible. To heal that loop in this lifetime, I would need to become peers with my father—to openly share ideas with him and have him accept my influence fully. This karmic loop has been resolved.

My grandmother and I: In that past life, my mother was teaching me healing techniques, and she lost her life because of it. To heal that karmic loop now, my grandmother would need to teach me once again, without fear of persecution. This loop was only partially healed, as she became a mentor for me as a spirit after her death. But while she was alive, family members discouraged her from teaching me anything, even though she and I both knew that I had spiritual gifts that needed to be honed and refined.

Each soul also had individual goals that they needed to work through that they'd brought from that lifetime into the current one. Although I am only fully sure of mine, I can hypothesize what the souls of my father and grandmother may have needed to resolve here.

My grandmother had a few key themes come up in that lifetime. First, she needed to find a partner whom she could trust implicitly. Unfortunately, this didn't happen for her. My grandmother married her best friend's boyfriend when she was very young because he was in the military and she needed to escape her home. Her father was involved in the mob in the Bronx, and my grandmother worried for her own safety, which turned out to be a valid fear. My grandfather, having married a woman he didn't love, cheated on her throughout their relationship. Their marital discord blocked my grandmother's ability to fully heal this aspect of herself.

Another important theme for my grandmother was to be able to practice her healing work freely, openly, and without fear of retribution. This was something she partially achieved. My grandmother was a renowned healer, using energy to heal ailments that were deemed incurable by the doctors of her patients. I lived with my grandmother during my early childhood, and I watched people come to her when they were sick, and after a few months of sessions, they would be healthy. I didn't realize it at the time, but her healing capabilities were incredibly profound. Her patients would call her an angel or a miracle worker, and I even heard an older woman refer to her as "the right hand of God." All the while, her family shunned her for her healing capabilities, calling her crazy and stating that her abilities were fabricated. I watched my grandmother wrestle with her family's judgment until she passed.

For as much good as my grandmother did for others, she and my grandfather were also incredibly toxic for their children. My father grew up in a home where he felt unsafe and unprotected; he was often left in dangerous situations from a young age or was expected to be the parent for his young parents. He recalls being left at baseball practice miles from home and having to walk home in the dark as a young child. He has recounted stories of bill collectors and angry tenants from his father's building threatening him when he was not yet ten years old. His chaotic childhood made it incredibly difficult for him to trust those around him, and it is a wound that he is currently attempting to heal now in his adulthood.

My father also has a soul theme of needing to let go of fear, of no longer allowing it to control his decisions as he did in that lifetime. Fear is highly motivating for my father after the childhood he had. The fear he experienced in the early part of this lifetime reinforced the fear that he felt in his past life, making it that much harder to overcome. I watch him now as he attempts to balance between acting from fear and acting from alignment, and which side wins varies, depending on the issue.

That lifetime brought up my soul's need to have independence, to make decisions that might be scary to others, but with trust in my own judgment to guide me. This is something I continually work toward, but I often go too far in the other direction, doing things out of spite rather than because I know in my gut that they're right. This is clearly a remnant of my past life, when I wanted to act in opposition to my father. Luckily, I have a husband who is keenly aware of this, and he does his best to remind me to come back into alignment.

Another theme that lifetime brought up for me was a fear of being a healer, as it could obviously mean ostracism or even death. It took me until my thirties to fully come out as a healer, leaving my identity as a psychotherapist (a well-respected, trusted, and safe career) behind to step into my role as a full-time healer.

When doing shadow work, a number of themes may begin to emerge within your family that become increasingly apparent the deeper you dive into your shadow. You may find that they tie back to your life lens, as generations of family members perpetuate the same struggles throughout their own lives, passing them down to the next generation when they fail to be healed. Since families travel throughout lifetimes together in soul pods, it is likely that you have all been experiencing these same issues repeatedly throughout many of your past lives, with each new lifetime offering an opportunity to correct the karmic loops you are entangled in.

As you explore your own inner world, begin to take note of the broad themes you can see within your lineage. You may want to ask yourself about the hardships your family has faced, the stories they tell, and the moments that stand out to you, and see if there is a common thread among them. This approach can guide you as you begin your own past life–focused shadow work, as you can identify the moments in past lives that set these future issues in motion.

Learning the Lessons of Our Past

When we encounter our past lives, certain moments are revealed to us because our souls need us to learn from those moments to grow. We are dropped into certain lifetimes and not others, or even into certain pivotal moments and not others, for a reason. Those lifetimes and those moments are important for us in the here and now, and altering how our body responds to them, while simultaneously learning the lesson, changes things dramatically for us in our present lives. Doing this provides us with the opportunity to heal moments at their source, creating a ripple effect of healing that transcends time.

When we are unable to heal something in one lifetime and it repeats in the lifetimes that follow, this is called a *karmic loop*. Karmic loops continue to repeat until healed because they represent a lesson that our soul needs to encounter and learn from. And once they've been fully healed through a full rewiring of neural pathways and physiological responses, they no longer trigger us in the present.

Earlier I mentioned a past life that I had in Scotland when I was the head witch of a coven. In my first recollection of that life, I witnessed the execution of a supposed witch, a young woman who had been an apprentice of mine. Through past life work, it was discovered that the young woman in that lifetime is my current biological sister, Monica, and the two of us are playing out a karmic loop from that lifetime.

When we accessed that past life connection, Monica and I recognized an area where our relationship needed to grow if we were to be released from that karmic loop. Monica has been following me since she was a young child. To alter this karmic loop, she needed to learn how to move away from my leadership and step into her own. Although acknowledging this pattern is a huge step, the next part has admittedly been harder for us both: breaking away from that pattern for good so that we can end this karmic loop once and for all.

The reason past life work is so profound for our own healing journeys is because experiences from our past lives constitute most of the information stored in the unconscious mind. Think about how much information you remember from your current lifetime. Reflect for a moment on the struggles and hardships you are fully conscious of and imagine how many more are buried away in your unconscious. It's a lot of information, right? Now multiply that by hundreds—because the number of past lives you have had is vast, and your brain still has access to memories from all of them within your unconscious mind.

Considering the amount of mental real estate past lives take up, you can imagine how much of who we are is based on versions of us that we have no recollection of. This means our personalities, behaviors, and current experiences are all being shaped by our immense past. When we use shadow work to return to our past lives, the amount of information we can exhume is infinite—and wildly healing, because it is often the root of patterns and problems that are occurring in this current lifetime.

Very often when I do shadow work with people, their minds naturally regress to past lives without any prompting, because the brain recognizes that this is the quickest way to heal from long-term issues. By reliving and rewiring the original cause of a broader issue, you can alter your human experience drastically in just moments.

Past lives are a key aspect of what is tucked away within the depths of your unconscious mind, but there are other key pieces of information that we can access when we traverse this space. In the next chapter, we'll continue exploring other unconscious material that you are likely to encounter while doing shadow work.

8

What Lurks in the Shadow

You know by now that shadow work is a broad term for the practice of engaging with anything existing in the unconscious mind. But what you might not know is exactly what type of information you will find when you begin to explore your shadow. Healing the unconscious has many different facets, all held underneath the larger umbrella term of *shadow work*. Some examples are inner child healing, womb work, ancestral healing, and past life work. Since we covered past life work extensively in the last chapter, in this chapter we'll dive into each of the other topics to uncover what these branches of shadow work entail. Remember that shadow work is not limited to these themes, and your experience can be as broad as you would like it to be. But these topics encompass many of the experiences we uncover through the process of shadow work, and a basic understanding of what they are and how they happen can be helpful on your shadow work journey.

Healing Your Inner Child

In the early 1900s, a Swiss psychologist named Jean Piaget developed the basis for our current understanding of the developmental stages of children. What he found was that before the age of six, children are quite egocentric. Seeing the world as if it revolves around them is a very normal experience for children this young, and it has to do with the brain's wiring system and capacities before this point. Piaget called this the Preoperational Stage, a time when we are ripe for internalizing trauma.

Piaget's discovery is exemplified perfectly in a psychological study he created that is referred to as the Three Mountain Task. In this test, children are seated in front of a model of three mountains. The mountains are each distinctly different from one another so that they are easily discernable for the children in the study. Before they are seated, the children can explore every side of the model by walking around it to observe the different angles. After they walk around and have seen all vantage points, they are seated in front of the model, and a doll is placed in a different location. The children are then shown photographs of that doll's potential perspective and asked which one most closely represents the perspective that the doll sees. Before age six, children consistently respond to this question by choosing the picture that shows the child's current viewpoint, meaning they don't understand that the doll would see something different from what they see, even though they and the doll are viewing the mountain from different vantage points. By age seven or eight, the children could clearly understand and answer the question correctly, showing that they understood that the doll would have a different perspective from theirs.

If children are egocentric, it means that they are unable to see other people's perspectives and instead focus on their own point of view. As highlighted in the Three Mountain Task, the perspective-taking limitation of young children is important because it exemplifies just how much they are unable to see things from another's point of view. This means that in any issue they encounter, regardless of whether it's about them or not, they will blame themselves, because they will be able to see it only from their own perspective and won't be able to factor in evidence to the contrary. As you can imagine, children witness a lot of potentially traumatic things at a young age, and their propensity to internalize these moments can lead to an abundance of unconscious trauma being stored within the shadow.

When doing inner child work, the goal is to heal the child that lies deep within the psyche. We all long for the days of our youth, when life was simple and we didn't govern ourselves with rules. Through shadow work, you can access the early moments that altered your once-innocent worldview to repair and restore the psyche. Doing so rewires neural pathways that are based on your earliest experiences, and it has a ripple effect of healing, altering your adult worldview.

One of the most prominent and impactful traumas that children can encounter at a young age is an attachment injury. Attachment is a phenomenon that was discovered by a researcher named Harry Harlow in the 1950s. Harlow conducted a study in which he separated infant rhesus monkeys from their mothers and placed them in one of two scenarios to explore the connection they might feel to a mother. The infant monkeys were placed either with a surrogate mother made entirely of wire that had the capacity to feed the monkeys with a bottle, or with a surrogate mother made of wire that was wrapped in soft terrycloth material but had no food. The goal behind the study was to see which surrogate mother the monkeys desired to be with: the surrogate mother who provided food or the surrogate mother who provided comfort. The result of the study was that the monkeys spent almost all of their time with the terrycloth mother, returning to the wire mother only when they were hungry and then immediately retreating to the cloth mother. And when something potentially frightening was placed in the cage, they would quickly return to the soft terrycloth mother for comfort.

What this study displayed was that infant rhesus monkeys preferred safety and comfort over all else, a result that surprised researchers because the theory before this was that basic survival needs would win out over attachment and comfort. This result was the beginning of attachment theory. The monkeys chose to spend time with their attachment figure (mother) for safety and comfort, which is exactly what we see in children. Researcher John Bowlby elaborated on Harlow's work with the development of his maternal deprivation hypothesis, which stated that disruptions in the care of a child by their primary attachment figure (typically mom) often results in long-term deficits and internalized trauma in the child.

Attachment is the basis for how we have related to other human beings throughout our lives. When we are children, we learn to connect to our primary attachment figure, and they become our safe base from which to explore the world. As we get older, if we've had a strong attachment, we create more and more space between ourselves and our primary attachment figure because we know they will always be there for us. That level of trust and safety enables us to move through the world curiously and without hesitation. When an attachment injury occurs, something has threatened that safety and caused the child to feel as though they have to be more cautious as they navigate the world. If the attachment injury is egregious, it could lead to marked personality and behavioral changes, making the child fearful, anxious, avoidant, or a combination of those three (this is called disorganized attachment).

While doing inner child work, the mission is to go back to the moments when someone experienced an attachment injury and help them to reexperience that injury through a different lens. The body is kept calm and neutral, breathing is regulated, and thoughts are monitored as those early moments are navigated. When we access these moments of attachment injury, we can interrupt the subconscious feedback loop to permanently change how these memories are stored within our systems. Doing so creates a domino effect of healing, as our later moments that were based on those attachment injuries become altered, too.

It's important to note that things that are traumatic for a child might not always be traumatic for an adult. For instance, the experience of a child whose parents forget to pick them up after school might be quite traumatic for that child. They might feel forgotten, abandoned, and terrified of being alone. If this same circumstance were to happen to an adult, the emotions would be much less intense. When you do inner child work, you may often find that you don't consider these early moments traumatic. But what is important here is that your inner child does, which means that your brain does as well. And because the brain has deemed these moments to be traumatic, the neural pathways that have been laid down in response are wired for heightened levels of arousal and fear, which has altered how you see the world as an adult.

Inner Child Healing Letter

Write a letter to your inner child. Your inner child lives within your physical body, and they have likely felt neglected for a long time. In this exercise, you are going to write a letter to your inner child as if you were writing a letter to any small child, such as your own child or a niece or nephew. Visualize yourself when you were young and explain the following:

- How much you love them unconditionally
- Any situations or circumstances from their childhood that you wish you could take back or change in some way, and why
- Ways that you can protect them now
- How you would like to spend time with them going forward (playing, meditating, etc.)

When writing this letter, think about it as telling yourself what you wish you had heard from your caregivers while growing up. What things could they have said to make you feel more loved and secure? Write them down here so that your inner child feels that level of connection and attachment to the adult version of you as you begin the process of healing your inner child.

Repeat this exercise as often as you like, and notice how you feel during and after you are done. Then be sure to follow through on the promise you made to spend time with your inner child, doing things like spending time outside playing in the grass, being creative and messy, or eating ice cream for dinner. Any activity that might help your inner child heal will be incredibly healing for you as an adult.

SAMPLE INNER CHILD LETTER

Dear Danielle,

You are compassionate, brave, and stronger than you can even imagine. I have always loved you and will continue to do so throughout your existence. There is nothing that you can do that would ever make you bad or wrong in my eyes. I hope you know that the love I have for you is infinite.

I'm so sorry that you have felt unworthy. All of the moments when the adults around you have made you feel like you weren't good enough were not your fault. Those moments were a reflection of them, not you. The pain and sadness that they felt was placed on your shoulders, and that never should have been yours to carry. Let me take these burdens away from you, my love. Let me remove them so you no longer feel unworthy and you remember just how powerful you are. Even though you are young, you are already so special. And I'm proud of everything you have accomplished so far.

Remember when your teacher told you that you were lazy? That you would never amount to anything because, despite being smart, you were bound to waste your talent? That wasn't true. You are not lazy, and you never were. What that teacher didn't see was how tired you were from being bullied. How you were trying to hold it all together while your classmates ripped you apart. You were doing extraordinarily well, and no one, especially the teacher, had any right to judge you for what you were going through. You were trying your best, and that is all anyone could ever ask of you.

You are strong. You are powerful. You have wisdom well beyond your age. Never let anyone ever make you feel unworthy again, because I am here to tell you that the only person who gets to define your worth is you.

From this point forward, I vow to protect you. If anyone tries to make you feel "less than" or unworthy, I will come to your defense immediately. I'll keep you safe by surrounding you with people who see your worth and by creating a boundary around you to keep you safe from those who are unable to. I vow to spend time with you every day. I will visit you during meditation and take you to that park you always loved to spend time at. We will play together, running around in the fresh air and spending time with my children, who are excited to be with you. And I vow to be the attachment figure you always deserved.

Love,
Danielle

When we connect with our inner child, we begin to shift our internalized attachments from other people around us to ourselves. We become our primary attachment figure, and we learn how to best reparent ourselves, providing for our inner child the unconditional love and support that we needed growing up.

Doing this shifts our perspective immensely by creating a level of safety that we didn't have when we were children, and this safety alters our neural pathways permanently to allow us to easily shift our current perspectives in adulthood. Everything about who we thought we were can change with inner child work because our personalities are not set in stone, and this work, in particular, can create new subconscious feedback loops based on our new experiences.

Womb Work

Although most modalities of shadow work do not seem gendered, womb healing implies that it is specific to those who have a uterus. However, that is *not* the case, as we all have a sacral chakra, the energetic center that womb healing refers to. This is an important distinction, because those with male organs can still greatly benefit from healing the sacral chakra, the energetic center responsible for the creation of *all* things, whether they be ideas, businesses, or children. Or someone might no longer have a uterus for any number of reasons, whether it be because of a hysterectomy or a gender reassignment surgery; nevertheless, the energetic womb remains. What that means is that even when we lose an organ, the energetic imprint of that organ remains. Long story short: absolutely everyone can benefit from womb work.

Womb healing is an ancient practice that centers on healing any unconscious information that may be stored within the energetic womb space. Think of the womb as the center of creation in your energetic body. From the womb, all things are created, whether they be children, businesses, relationships, or ideas; they all stem from the sacral chakra and are later birthed into life.

Remember that all unconscious trauma is stored in the body, because the physical body doesn't have the ability to repress information the way the mind does. Thus, traumas that implant themselves in the energetic womb space can lead to issues like dysmenorrhea, premenstrual dysphoric disorder, endometriosis, or even cancer (cervical, ovarian, or uterine) for women, or issues like lower back pain, issues with libido/desire, and urine/kidney problems for all people. These issues are an indication that something is awry in the energetic womb space, and womb work is one way in which that stored trauma can be released from this area.

Historically, women have faced more trauma than men because of being oppressed or used for sex, though this is not something that happens exclusively to women. And when events such as those occur, remnants of the traumas remain hidden in the unconscious mind and the energetic womb space, affecting the survivor's ability to live and function normally. When left untreated for long periods, issues arising from events such as those listed above are likely to persist. And because of the current medical model of treatment, doctors rarely make the connection between trauma and these physical symptoms, meaning most people may be medicated long term to quiet the symptoms of their sacral chakra imbalance, and they don't ever get to the root of the problem. As you can imagine, this often leads to long-term complications.

During shadow work intended to heal womb traumas, the goal is to return to the moment those traumas occurred and to alter the reaction to them, permanently interrupting the subconscious feedback loop that currently exists and replacing it with a new one that helps alleviate the pain of the initial trauma. When this is done, the trauma is released from this physical and energetic center, allowing the energy of the sacral chakra to return to alignment and alleviating any physical symptoms that were present to alleviate.

My cancer was exacerbated by several "big T" and "little t" traumas that were stored in the energetic womb space. The warning signs were all present: horrifically painful menstrual cycles, atypical periods, irregular digestion, shingles, constant lower back pain, hypersexuality, and more. It was all there, right in front of me, but it was consistently ignored and disregarded by my doctors and me. After ignoring these warning signs for decades and being exposed to other contributing factors that increased my likelihood of developing cervical cancer, I created a toxic environment in my body where cancer was able to thrive. After doing womb-centered shadow work, I have been able to fully heal this energetic center.

Everything Is Energy

Issues with the sacral chakra often result from an imbalance in divine masculine and divine feminine energy, the result of repressed trauma stored in this energetic space. When I say masculine and feminine, I don't mean that men have masculine energy and women have feminine energy. In fact, we all have both, and they are meant to be a perfectly even balance within us all. Rather than thinking about divine masculine and divine feminine energy as opposites, consider them two equally important parts of a greater energetic whole. To keep our sacral chakras running smoothly, an even balance of divine masculine and divine feminine energy is required. Although ideally we want our energies to be in balance with one another, most of us lean on one energy type more than another as the direct result of experiences we have had throughout our current and past lifetimes. That preference can tilt us out of alignment and make it difficult to achieve true balance within ourselves.

Divine masculine energy is action-oriented, disciplined, decisive, boundaried, confident, logical, and organized. When it's in balance with feminine energy, those with these qualities are excellent leaders. When there is an excess of masculine energy, it can lead to a domineering nature, aggression, and an intense need for control. Those with too much masculine behavior often sabotage relationships and become disconnected from their internal state.

Divine feminine energy is empathic, creative, wise, nurturing, and highly intuitive. When balanced with the power of the divine masculine, divine feminine energy allows a person to effortlessly flow with their creations and bring any idea to life. When there is an imbalance of too much feminine energy without its masculine counterpart, it can lead to feelings of depression, isolation, fear, desperation, and exhaustion, along with feelings of being stuck.

There is a special type of power that comes from finding the perfect balance of these two energies. It enables those with this balance to manifest quite easily, as they can access all of the best aspects of themselves, not to mention the obvious health benefits of keeping this chakra in alignment. Here is an exercise you can use to diagnose your energy and learn how to bring your divine masculine and divine feminine into balance.

Diagnosing and Aligning Your Energy

Begin by reading the following descriptions and seeing which most closely describes you.

TOO MUCH DIVINE MASCULINE ENERGY:
What it looks like: You are a natural-born leader and take the position with pride. But you often take on too much, struggling with work-life balance. However, you rarely even notice the imbalance, as

you don't mind overworking. Others look to you as a problem solver because you don't let emotions get in the way of your decision-making process and can choose what is best quickly and decisively. You rarely receive help from others; you feel they will disappoint you, and when others do attempt to assist you, they often leave you feeling disappointed—you feel you would have done a better job yourself. Others may describe you as Type A, overbearing, workaholic, or controlling.

The imbalance: When too much masculine energy is present without the balance of its feminine counterpart, you will likely feel overworked and isolated. The hustle mindset that you're stuck in is stopping you from leaning into your creativity and flow, which means you have tunnel vision. Being hyperfocused on goals can mean that you are out of touch with yourself and disconnected from your emotions, which leads to higher levels of anxiety. You may even unintentionally self-sabotage and cause chaos in your life any time things feel too peaceful.

How to create balance: Those with too much masculine energy need to learn to slow down and receive. After doing womb-focused shadow work to home in on the energy of your sacral chakra, begin to incorporate the following into your routine:

- Start a gratitude journal.
- Say yes when people offer you things.
- Learn to delegate tasks that you don't enjoy.

⬤ Have a daily meditation practice to help
you slow down and get in touch with your
inner wisdom.

TOO MUCH DIVINE FEMININE ENERGY:

What it looks like: You consider yourself a true
empath, absorbing other people's emotions like
a sponge. You may have a tendency to jump to
conclusions or craft stories in your mind without
attempting to gain clarity on situations. You tend
to give more than others in relationships and often
feel as if you're the one making all the effort. When
you have an idea that you desire to act on, you
have trouble getting clear on the steps you need
to take and end up getting stuck in idea mode.
Others may describe you as being needy, emotional, or overly sensitive.

The imbalance: When too much feminine
energy is present without the balance of its masculine counterpart, you likely feel out of alignment.
Although you are in touch with your emotions,
your tendency to absorb them from other people
can disrupt your energetic flow. You may spend a
lot of time ruminating on things that have occurred
in the past rather than staying focused on the
present moment. This imbalance can cause you to
overwork emotionally, especially in relationships
and in business, but without feeling as if you ever
gain much traction in moving forward.

How to create balance: Even though your emotions have been your guide in the past, it is time to

begin listening primarily to your intuition instead, allowing your emotions to inform rather than lead. After doing shadow work focused on the womb, begin adding the following things into your routine:
- ◕ Journaling
- ◕ Volunteering for organizations or charities that you care about
- ◕ Taking yourself out on dates
- ◕ Creating yearly, monthly, and weekly goals to follow through on, with a carefully laid out plan to achieve them

By getting to the root of your traumas that are housed in your womb space and working to align your divine masculine and feminine energies at this center, you will undoubtedly begin to feel more at peace with yourself. Womb work helps you to feel aligned and energized, enabling you to access all aspects of yourself on your journey forward.

Ancestral Healing

My husband Andrew's maternal grandfather, Ernie, immigrated from Italy in the early 1900s. Although I was never able to meet him (he passed away just before I met my husband in 2006), Ernie lived on in the stories that his four daughters enjoyed sharing about him. They painted a picture of a beautiful soul: someone who was generous, kind, warm, and unbelievably selfless. The man in these stories is someone I wish I'd had a chance to meet in person, because according to anyone you ask, he was truly remarkable.

One story about him that always stuck out to me was about the early years after Ernie and his family first immigrated to America. This was a different type of story from the ones the sisters typically shared, because they weren't privy to many of the details of Ernie's early life. The story goes that after immigrating to America, Ernie's family spent a few years working together on a small farm in Vineland, New Jersey, as they attempted to save up enough money to make their way in a new country. After working long, laborious days on the farm, the family would all sleep together in what they called the "employee shed," a minute structure with small folding cots that they would rest on at night. The cots were stiff and didn't have a mattress, which meant they provided no additional warmth for comfort.

The conditions on the farm were brutal, and the family had to be careful to remain safe, especially during the colder months. Ernie was about ten years old when a tragic accident occurred that altered the course of his and his family's life forever.

At the end of the workday, Ernie was walking back from the farm toward the employee shed with his older brother, Luigi, on a particularly hot day. Luigi, who was about twelve years old, decided to have a moment of playful, childlike freedom and go for a swim in a small lake on the outskirts of the farm. Ever the cautious one, Ernie urged Luigi not to go, since the night would be cold; but Luigi didn't listen, instead allowing himself to indulge in a rare moment of unbridled freedom.

That evening, Luigi was freezing. He was shivering so forcefully that it woke up Ernie, who attempted to warm his older brother by lying on top of him. After a horrific night, Luigi became extremely ill, running a dangerously high fever and displaying many of the symptoms of pneumonia, such as shallow breathing and a terrible cough. Ernie's mother carried her son's limp body across the fields to the owner of the farm, begging him to take them to the hospital, where Luigi tragically died shortly after they arrived.

The tragic loss of his brother had a lasting impact on Ernie, causing him to perpetually be afraid of losing his family. In fact, his daughters have also shared stories from their own childhood in which their father would wake them up from sleep to make sure that they were safe. His deep-rooted concern for their safety and fear for their lives stemmed from this early childhood trauma.

This story has remained with me because it explained so many of the personality traits and behaviors that I witnessed in Ernie's daughters and his grandchildren. On a behavioral level, my husband's family is fiercely protective of one another, and they are more supportive of each other than any other family I have ever come into contact with. If someone is sick, everyone becomes a caretaker, rushing to the side of the person in need immediately upon hearing the news. But even more striking is how each family member has higher than normal levels of chronic anxiety that are intensely exacerbated by illness, no matter how slight the illness might be. And as we know, chronic anxiety is the leading cause of illness, so this loop that the family becomes entangled in is cyclical and infinite, with their chronic stress leading to illness and the illness itself causing more stress and anxiety.

What Is Ancestral Healing?

Ancestral healing is the ancient practice of healing the wounds carried down through bloodlines. Although that may sound like a pseudoscience, there is actually solid scientific data being acquired today that reinforces our understanding of how our genes carry information from one generation to the next. The field of science that studies how genes are expressed is called *epigenetics*, and epigenetics studies how trauma that is hidden away in the shadow affects the expression of our genes.

Our bodies are made up of genetic codes called *deoxyribonucleic acid*, or DNA, and the way these genes are expressed can vary from person to person. In studies of identical twins, researchers have found that two identical twins can end up looking significantly physically different based on their environment. These studies often monitor identical twins who have grown up in separate homes, often because they have been adopted by two different families, so the twins can be raised in tremendously different environments. The twins in these studies have the exact same DNA, but the expression of this DNA can vary greatly based on how they were nurtured by the people around them, as well as by their environment. What this means is that our ecosystem can cause specific genes either to be turned on or off like a light switch. Some gene expression can change over time if the environment is altered.

According to research, trauma does not cause a change in our genetics, but rather causes a change in our epigenetics, altering how specific genes are expressed. These changes are passed down to our offspring and continue through our bloodlines until someone alters this progression by healing the root cause of the altered gene expression. The trauma we experience is passed down through generations, causing specific issues such as higher risks for obesity, disease, anxiety, and even death.

Although the field of epigenetics is relatively new, dating back only a few decades, ample evidence can already be seen to support these claims. And as collective traumas such as 9/11 and the COVID-19 pandemic continue to be studied, many more specifics will be uncovered about how potent trauma can be for gene expression passed down through generations of families.

When attempting to heal your bloodline through ancestral healing, the focus of the shadow work is on recalling memories that extend beyond your own consciousness by tapping into what is known as the *collective unconscious*. The collective unconscious is the deepest level of your unconscious mind, passed down to you from your ancestors, and it houses your most deep-rooted fears and beliefs. Carl Jung, who coined the phrase *collective unconscious*, believed that these ancestral roots went so deep that they affected all humans globally in similar ways. Jung postulated that some similarities and universal beliefs that we all share, such as morals, are evidence of the reach of the collective unconscious.

Through ancestral healing, you can recall moments from the history of your ancestors that forever changed them on a chemical level. These moments altered the expression of their DNA, which you now carry—so altering them in the present can rectify the chemical change of the gene expression in your current physical body.

As you might imagine, the process of ancestral healing can be wildly healing on many different levels. It can release profoundly deep-rooted fears that have been passed down through family bloodlines for generations, or even lessen your potential to develop certain illnesses, such as obesity or cancer.

In the case of my husband's family, the ancestral healing my husband, Andrew, has done has been to work on releasing the fear he carries that has been passed down through his own family's bloodline. Andrew has healed the subconscious feedback loop that existed within him and no longer suffers from chronic stress, theoretically altering the expression of his genes and those of the generation that has come after. If he healed them at the root (and let's hope that he has), our children's genes will express without any trauma markers.

Something wonderfully unexpected that has also come from Andrew's healing journey is how much it has affected his family members, as well. In the past five years, I have watched many of them slowly start to lessen their attachment to fear as they witness one of their own family doing things that they might previously have described as risky, such as when we moved more than three hours away for one year (the entire extended family lives within thirty minutes of one another). The more risks Andrew takes, the more he challenges the constructed narrative of the family, and the more opportunity exists for anyone within the extended family unit to challenge the norm. All it takes for ancestral healing to be effective is for one person to break the generational curses that exist in a bloodline. When that occurs, the ripple effects are profound.

9

Human Error

Believe it or not, I never intended to become an author. In fact, I opted out of pursuing my PhD because the thought of having to write another lengthy thesis seemed completely daunting. But in the spring of 2020, I met an Akashic records practitioner named Rebecca Lyons who changed my viewpoint entirely. In case you have never heard of the Akashic records before, I'll note that they are a collection of everything that has happened throughout the universe in the past, the present, and even the future (remember that time isn't as linear as we are led to believe).

Practitioners who work with the Akashic records can help you access important information about where your soul has been, how to align with your highest path in your current life, or how to retrieve potential future realities in the quantum field that are available to you. The Akashic records pair beautifully with shadow work, because both help you get to the core of issues that you may be struggling with and can help you heal from lifetimes of karma.

During our first Akashic records session, Rebecca told me that aligning with my highest path would mean that I would become a world-renowned author, penning not just one, but several books on shadow work. At first, I laughed. I couldn't help myself! How could the one thing I never wanted to accomplish be such an integral part of my soul's purpose in this life-time? I couldn't fathom this possibility, and although I wrote down her suggestion, I didn't take it very seriously. After seeing my reaction, Rebecca said that she was visualizing a book with the word *journal* on the cover. She thought it might be somewhere that I could start writing down ideas for future books, so I told her I would take that under advisement.

Because of my need to get to the root of my resis-tance to this idea, I began practicing shadow work to uncover the primary experience that led to this bodily reaction. What I found was a memory of myself as a child singing in front of my class, only to be teased by the teacher when I was done about how this wasn't my best performance. As I reexperienced the laughter of all the young students in the room joining in with my teacher mocking my failure, I felt overwhelmingly ashamed for not performing well. I was embarrassed, especially because my singing voice had been a source of pride and confidence for me until that moment. I watched my inner light dim as flashes of old memories swirled through my mind. These were of moments when I suppressed my voice to blend in, not draw attention, or when I was so afraid to not perform that I made myself do worse than I otherwise might have.

As I reexperienced these moments, I went back and healed them all. I gave myself the love and nurturing that I had needed the first time, and I altered my mind and body's reaction to each of those moments, replacing the initial reaction I'd had years ago with overwhelming love and encouragement. In an instant, I changed my fear of using my voice and created a new story within my energetic field about how my voice was and always will be my greatest asset.

I decided then to create a new story that would later form into a subconscious feedback loop. I decided to believe that not only was my voice powerful beyond measure, but also that it was needed in this world at this time. That my voice would awaken others to the power that they held within, and I could no longer afford to be silent. I began writing this book the next day.

Months into the writing, I felt disconnected from the process of using my journal. Having to transfer my written thoughts over to my computer became increasingly daunting, and I eventually abandoned the journal altogether. I forgot what Rebecca had said to me about the importance of a journal, and I stuck to typing my thoughts in various documents on my computer. I even starting using some of the individual thoughts that I'd received as downloads from my spirit guides to create social media content, which seemed to engage a lot of people who were curious about pursuing shadow work. One morning, I woke up with an idea: what if I were to create a book of shadow work prompts for people to use as they began their personal shadow work journey? I sat down at my computer, opened up a blank Word document, and let my fingers move over the keyboard. By that afternoon, I had written the book of prompts, created its cover design, and submitted it for self-publishing. It wasn't until it was formally released online that I realized what I had done. The book, called *The Shadow Seekers Journal*, was the journal that Rebecca had told me about when we accessed the Akashic records! It was never meant to be the place where I wrote down my ideas for my larger book. Rather, it was meant to be my *first book* of the many that I would release.

Our guides are always communicating with us; through cosmic breadcrumbs or through healing sessions like Akashic records and shadow work, the best path forward will become increasingly clear when we allow ourselves to listen. But listening is only half the battle, and overriding our body's desire to stay the same is the next challenge that needs to be faced.

Hacking Your Biology to Create Change from the Inside Out

Our behaviors, and even our lives as a whole, are just a series of patterns. Like a computer program, we are subconsciously running our programming on repeat until we decide to create a change. But to make that change stick, it's imperative to get to the root of how that pattern was created in the first place. That is where shadow work comes in.

With shadow work, we are diving into the unconscious mind to look for repressed emotions and memories that may be dictating our current behaviors and circumstances. Because any subconscious feedback loop that you're running—whether it's overeating, overspending, or falling for people who aren't good for you—is just a pattern that can be interrupted.

In the last year or so, how many times have you thought about changing something in your life? Maybe you have considered working on your relationship by going to couples therapy, or you have grandiose plans of getting into the best shape of your life. Maybe you have considered learning a new language or starting a business. Whatever these goals are that you have considered, I can guess what might happen next. After telling yourself all the reasons you want to do this, the voice of the ego steps in and tells you exactly why it isn't going to work for you. Maybe it's something like "you know that you don't have time to go to the gym," or "you are not smart enough to learn a new language." Maybe the ego voice has said to you, "couples therapy won't help your relationship—your partner doesn't like you enough to go," or "no one will ever want to work with you, so why bother trying to start a business that is doomed to fail?" You might even override this voice and begin anyway. But more often than not, these new pathways are eventually abandoned because the voice of the ego wins out over the potential growth you would experience from the unknown pathway.

The version of you that currently exists is safe. Within your current reality, your mind and body know exactly what to expect. There are few surprises; life is predictable, and it takes very little effort on the part of your physical system. That is an ideal situation for the mind and body, because staying exactly where you are is infinitely easier than becoming who you are meant to be. And creating any deviation from this path will require more effort than the mind and body are comfortable producing. This is exactly why the ego voice is there, as an evolutionary mechanism designed to keep you exactly as you are.

It's easier for the mind and body to maintain homeostasis and keep you on your path; it is energetically much more difficult to repress unconscious information and keep it sealed away safely within the unconscious mind. In fact, doing so over long periods exhausts the body, as trauma is stored within the physical system. When too much energy is devoted to repressing trauma, our immune systems are weakened, because we are in a state of constant stress. According to separate studies by the National Center for Biotechnology Information (NCBI) and the American Psychological Association (APA), chronic stress is the number-one cause of most physical and mental ailments. These include, but are not limited to, heart attack, stroke, autoimmune disease, cancer, and psychological disorders such as post-traumatic stress disorder, schizophrenia, dissociative identity disorder, ADHD, and personality disorders. In fact, an entire field has been developed, called *psychoneuroimmunology*, that is dedicated solely to the study of the effect of the mind on disease. What researchers in this field have found is that as unconscious information is repressed, chronic stress results, causing an immunosuppressive effect that affects the body's ability to prevent illness and disease.

Letting Go of Your Attachment to Who You Have Been

While the science clearly shows motivating factors for why shadow work is imperative, doing that work is often still easier said than done. Early on in this book, I stated that part of the reason that most people never grow is that they become too attached to who they are. Our unconscious experiences shape our personalities and behaviors, and we tell ourselves the lie that this is just who we are. This couldn't be further from the truth. When you do shadow work to rewire your early experiences, your personality and behaviors naturally begin to shift on their own. But if you want to create longstanding change, it is up to you to create new experiences to replace the old ones.

This is the moment when you have to choose to release the security blanket of your old reality in favor of the limitless potential of the quantum reality that lies before you. When the ego appears, remember that it is just part of the subconscious feedback loop designed to reinforce your old patterns, and *choose differently*. Replace those ego-based thoughts with powerful statements about who you know you will become as you access the quantum. Additionally, you can reinforce the new subconscious feedback loop even further if you think about experiences, emotions, and physical reactions that can accompany the new thought, leaving any guesswork out of the equation for the mind and body. Use the following exercise to design your new reality.

Overcoming the Ego

What ego messages came to your mind as you read this chapter? For instance, one ego message could be "you'll never change who you are; this is just your personality, and you are stuck with it." Use these ego messages, or any other prominent ones that you repeatedly hear, as you navigate this exercise.

On a piece of paper, write out the following prompts and the responses that come up for you. If you choose, you can hang them somewhere in your home so that you can see them each day (on a mirror, in your bedroom, and so on). This visual will serve as a daily reminder of the new subconscious feedback loop that you are creating.

Ego message one:

_____

Ego message two:

_____

Ego message three:

_____

Now choose how you plan to respond to that
ego message from this point forward. To continue
with my earlier example, the response might be "I
am constantly evolving and changing, growing into
the most aligned version of myself." The experiences, emotions, and physical reactions that will
reinforce this new subconscious feedback loop
could be to do something new every week, feeling pride and excitement as you do so. Pay close
attention to how it feels in your body each time
you accomplish a new feat. Add the following to
your journal page:

Response to ego message one:

_____

**What experiences, emotions, and physical
reactions will reinforce this new subconscious
feedback loop?**

_____

Response to ego message two:

_____

What experiences, emotions, and physical reactions will reinforce this new subconscious feedback loop?

_____

Response to ego message three:

_____

What experiences, emotions, and physical reactions will reinforce this new subconscious feedback loop?

_____

By reviewing your responses to these prompts each day, you'll be able to reprogram your ego messages through time and practice.

Once you have fully committed to incorporating these practices into your life, you will notice the voice of your ego changing. Although it will never fully retreat, you will notice it becoming more timid as the inner voice of your intuition becomes louder. As you evolve, this process will naturally shift with you. With each new goal, a new ego message will pop up to urge you to remain within your new levels of homeostasis. Keep this exercise in mind to continue to thwart these efforts, and to continue to grow exponentially.

Becoming the person you desire to be comes from the practice of rewriting the narratives your brain has chosen to subscribe to through the use of neural pathways. Through shadow work, you'll begin eradicating the neural pathways that support old ways of thinking, and with ego work, you will help solidify that process. Once the old neural pathways have been eliminated, new ones will be able to take a firm hold in your brain's circuitry, and you will begin to think, feel, and act like—and, in fact, be—the version of yourself that you truly wish to embody.

PART THREE

Becoming a
Shadow Seeker

10

Embracing the Shadow

As you know well by now, shadow work is the process of accessing the unconscious mind. This can be achieved in a multitude of ways, and these ways vary in their effectiveness. One popular method of doing shadow work is to use journal prompts to excavate the shadow and manage what is unearthed. Although this method is an easy entry point for most individuals on their shadow work journey, it's not as effective as other methods. The reason is that you are more likely to be accessing subconscious memories without truly eliciting information from the unconscious mind. Journaling is still helpful and effective for altering thoughts and behaviors, but other methods will help you access the unconscious at a deeper level.

The method that I find to be the most direct and helpful in accessing the unconscious is one I observed for myself during a past life regression session. I discovered this method by witnessing myself performing shadow work in this particular way in a past life, and in reexperiencing it there, I knew that I could bring it to this time and have it be helpful in my work now. I call this technique the Shadow Seekers Method, and it will allow you to easily reexperience moments that are tucked away in the unconscious. This approach will put you in the right place to interrupt and alter the subconscious feedback loop that those moments have created.

The Shadow Seekers Method

Here is how it works:

First, set the mood for your journey. Create a comfortable environment. Here is a list of things you can do to ensure success:

- Turn down any bright lights in the room.
- Lock the door so that you won't be interrupted.
- Turn off your phone and email notifications.
- Communicate to anyone around you that you are not to be interrupted during this meditation.
- Remove any jewelry or clothing items that might pull your attention, such as watches or glasses.
- Light candles or incense to create a peaceful space.
- Choose to lie down or sit up. Either is fine, but you will need to remain in whichever

position you choose for a while, so make sure that it is comfortable.

- Use any tools you enjoy interacting with in your own spiritual practice. For example, you may wish to incorporate crystals and essential oils.

When you have created a safe environment, begin to meditate to the point where you are walking the edge between waking and dreaming. This is the most important step in the process. When we meditate to this point, we are accessing what are called *theta brain waves*, which occur at about 4–7 Hz. A theta brain wave state allows us access to the unconscious mind while we are still in total control of our body and mind. You can move into this state by guiding yourself through a meditation, or by listening to one of my recorded meditations. Everyone is different, so trust whatever works best for you. You will know when you have achieved this point by how your body feels. If all parts of your body are completely relaxed and you feel as though you could easily drift off to sleep, you are there!

Call upon your spirit guides: When we traverse the unconscious mind, we will likely encounter information that the mind and body would deem intense. This is why we want to ensure that we are divinely led and fully protected on this journey. I recommend calling in whatever spirit guides you feel most comfortable with to assist you by asking them (out loud or in your mind) to be with you while you enter the shadow. Remember that, depending on how far into your spiritual journey you are, you may not see them. It could be a feeling or an inner knowing that they are there, or even something that you hear. Trust that however it is that they are coming through to you, they are with you.

Ask for help: Once you have brought your guides in, you can choose one of them to lead you to information that is for your highest and greatest good. When doing shadow work, we want to set the specific intention of healing something that is holding us back in our current life, and allow that intention to lead us to whatever moment our guides feel will be most helpful for us to tend to.

You may not know which guide it is that is leading you, and that is perfectly fine. Allow yourself to trust that whoever is coming through (as long as the energy they carry *feels good* to you) is there to lead you toward something that is helpful. If you don't know who the guide is, confirm by asking out loud, "Spirit, are you here for my highest and greatest good?" If they respond yes, continue on your journey. If they say no, order them to leave by saying out loud, "I do not consent to your presence here. Leave at once." When they are gone, choose a new guide.

Notice the details: During shadow work meditations, details are key. As your guide brings you toward whatever it is that you need to see, pay attention, using all your senses. Take in the smells, textures, colors, and so on, allowing the information to be rich in detail. The stronger the memory is, the stronger the neural rewiring will be.

Monitor your body: As you move closer to the moment that you need to reexperience, you will notice a reaction in your body. You may feel your heart beating faster, your palms becoming sweaty, or any other physical response that indicates that your autonomic nervous system is activated. The moment you notice this occurring, bring your attention to your breath. Allow yourself to calm your body down, reminding it that you are completely safe in this moment and no harm can come to you.

When your body is fully relaxed once more, continue your journey. Allow yourself to relive the traumatic moment. While reexperiencing something that was traumatic for you in the past, it is imperative that your body remain calm. Remember that your breath is medicine and use it to calm your nervous system. Witness what you came here to see, and experience it from a place of total calm and relaxation.

Ask your guides questions: If there is anything you wish to know about the moment you are witnessing, allow your spirit guide to act as a sort of tour guide. Ask them questions and allow them to answer. There is no limit to the number of questions that you can ask, and you should stay until you feel as though you received everything you came for.

When you have fully witnessed all that you need to see, allow everything around you to fade away, until only you and your spirit guide are together, surrounded by white light. Ask yourself out loud, "Where has this moment been living in my body?" and scan for discomfort or pain. It may feel slight, but it could also be intense. The body has been carrying this for a long time. Once you know where the trauma has been stored physically, ask your spirit guide to place their hands on that part of your body and to pull the darkness out of you completely. Watch all of it being removed until there is nothing left. When this process is complete, slowly allow yourself to come back to your physical body by bringing your awareness to where you are lying or sitting. Start to wiggle your fingers and toes and slowly open your eyes.

The final step is to journal everything that you experienced.

Shadow work is best practiced on a regular basis, which I would argue is once per week when you begin, slowly decreasing your sessions as you find greater levels of peace within your life. That timeline may vary based on how much you are repressing within your shadow. If you want to practice more frequently to accelerate your healing, that is fine too; however, sessions should be spaced at least two to three days apart, to allow your body and mind time to fully integrate the healing from your previous session.

When you begin using shadow work as a regular part of your life, you'll notice that things begin to shift, both internally and externally, in your world. As you remove the root source of your triggers, you will have a more even temperament. Situations that were once potentially triggering for you will be met with ease, as your body no longer responds in the same way to those types of experiences. And as within, so without; your external world will begin to change along with your internal state.

When your body and mind begin to react differently, you begin showing up differently in the world. You'll be calmer, more confident, and more open to receiving. As this happens, the people around you will need to accommodate this shift, either by growing with you or by removing themselves if they can't be part of your growth journey. As the people around you become aligned with the new version of you, you will find that new experiences present themselves as well. To be clear, experiences like this may have presented themselves before, but you were too triggered to receive them, or you may have let them pass by because of limiting beliefs like feelings of unworthiness.

As you begin to open yourself up to new experiences, you will solidify new neural pathways and bodily reactions around feelings of worthiness, confidence, and acceptance. And these are precisely the type of subconscious feedback loops that can bring your manifestations to life.

Remember that we remarked earlier that for a manifestation to come to fruition, you need to be fully open to receive it on every sensory level. You need to know what this new thing feels like, smells like, looks like, and so on. You need it to be so vivid in your mind and body that your physical and energetic systems already believe that you have it. Because when you align with this future reality on a quantum level, the universe co-conspires to bring this alternate reality forward with no hesitation.

Making Your Dreams a Reality

After doing my shadow work sessions to rid myself of the fear of using my voice, I began to write this book. I didn't know what I would do with it. I just knew that I had to begin to get it out of my head and on paper. I used all the tools I've described in this book, and I began to manifest a book contract. I visualized so clearly the image of the book in bookstores around the globe. I saw myself walking into Barnes & Noble and seeing it on a table by the entrance. I felt myself holding it in my hands, with tears in my eyes as I flipped through the pages that I had written. I saw myself at book signings connecting with the people who would be ready to dive into the shadow with everything they had, to completely alter their realities and access the quantum. And one year after beginning this process, I received a call from my future publisher asking me if I would write a book about how to use shadow work.

The ultimate secret to unlocking the life of your dreams is this: *you must become more than your mind and body.* The moment you can zoom out and see all of these unconscious processes happening before your eyes, you'll recognize that you are so much more than who you have been taught that you are. You are pure divine consciousness. You are a light being. You are a soul housed in a body, floating on a rock hurtling through space, here to learn the lessons that will help your soul elevate that divine consciousness. And truthfully? The stuff you normally bog yourself down with doesn't matter, because when you realize how powerful you are, you will see the programming that you're running and understand how to stop and alter it with ease.

Everything you have experienced, in this life and your past lives, has led you to this moment of total awareness. And it's up to you to internalize this lesson and let it empower you to create the life of your dreams.

Absolutely anything is possible when you heal your shadow, because doing so makes you limitless. And when you partner shadow work with manifestation, your dreams will become your reality. Needless to say, when I told my Akashic records practitioner Rebecca about this book being published, she was truly excited to say "I told you so!"

11

Bringing It Home

Every one of you has an integrated, embodied, holistic version of yourself within that is dying to get out. This very real potential you is trapped under layers of consciousness, screaming at you through your body to hear them, to listen closer, and to do something to help them out of the darkness that they are stuck in. Although they are trapped down there, you're up here, wishing your life looked different. Hoping for the answer to show up on your doorstep and free you from the confines of the life that you have but wish that you didn't. But the funny thing is, every moment that you spend wishing and hoping and dreaming for a different version of yourself to emerge, this aligned version of you is wishing and hoping and dreaming the exact same thing. And it is up to you to make the conscious choice to use everything you have learned to fully excavate them from the shadows, bring them into your conscious awareness, and merge the two of you. When you do, you will finally have full capability to create your dream life. Just remember a few important facts:

Shadow work is not for the faint of heart.

Within the shadow are all the moments that your mind has repressed out of fear for your fragile psyche. Your traumas, your heartbreaks, your past lives, your wounds all still exist within you, hidden out of sight within the unconscious mind. Keeping all of that unstable cognitive material locked away within the unconscious causes significant changes to the subconscious, altering your personality and your behaviors semi-permanently (and for many, permanently), until you make the decision to willingly brave the unconscious to face those moments head-on so that they can be healed for good.

Shadow work is going to send you into a tailspin.

Your mind and body truly want nothing more than to remain at their current level of homeostasis. Wherever you are today, mentally, physically, emotionally, and energetically, that is exactly where your mind and body would like to keep you, because maintaining homeostasis requires very little effort. The process of creating change can be unbelievably taxing on your various internal systems. And even though it may be exactly what you want, your mind and body will do absolutely anything to prevent you from creating growth.

This means that your mind and body are going to kick into overdrive to stop you from becoming the next version of yourself. Your mind will increase the amount of negativity it sends your way, sending you intrusive thoughts and lower limiting beliefs, and kick-starting the freeze response of the autonomic nervous system to cause you to halt your efforts. Your body will react to the freeze response, moving blood and oxygen away from the muscles and organs within your body that need it most to help you push through. You'll feel weak, lethargic, and frightened.

Many people take these responses as a sign that they should stop. But after reading this book, you now understand that this is exactly the moment when you need to double down on your commitment to growth. If you can interrupt the subconscious feedback loops designed to keep you stuck, you can create exponential growth that exceeds your wildest dreams.

Shadow work is not easy.

The process of reexperiencing your most difficult moments is terrifying and not something that should be taken lightly. To face your shadow means acknowledging that there are significant changes that you want to make along the way to becoming who you were always meant to be and knowing that, although the process may be frightening and may hurt temporarily, facing the shadow is the best way to completely release yourself from all of the emotional, mental, and energetic weight holding you back.

Even though shadow work is difficult, there are many ways to practice shadow work that will help you feel safe, held, and guided through the process. One of these is to rely on your spirit guides for help as you navigate the shadow. Connecting with your spirit guides helps you throughout the process of shadow work, because your guides will walk with you every step of the way, ensuring that you see only what will be helpful for you on your shadow work journey and answering any questions that you may have along the way. The other, and most important, way to protect yourself during shadow work is to get really good at listening to your body. Your body is fully aware of absolutely everything your soul has ever experienced. This means it is in a unique position to tell you what you need during the practice of shadow work, acting like a kinesthetic guide as you progress through the depths of the unconscious. Your body will alert you when the moments that need healing are close at hand, and it will react abruptly when there is something that needs healing. Learn to speak your body's language and allow it to be your most valuable resource on your shadow work journey.

Shadow work is the missing piece in the manifestation process.

Once you have fully removed from your shadow the pivotal, defining moments that have been stopping you from moving forward with your life, the process of manifestation becomes significantly easier. To bring future potential realities to life, all you have to do is bring them into the present moment. And without any material from the shadow blocking your path toward that new potential reality, you only need to reach out and grab it.

Decide what the life that you want to lead looks like. Not the one people have told you that you should want or the one you see being portrayed through media, religion, or various other contexts. What is it that *you really want*? Get crystal clear on that vision. Become familiar with how it feels, smells, tastes, and sounds. How will you feel when it is finally yours? When you see yourself living that life, knowing that you were the one who made it happen, what emotions arise? When you know your future so intimately that it is as if you already have it, keep living there in your mind, body, and energy. Then it is only a matter of time before it is officially yours.

Shadow work is the answer your soul has been searching for.

The entirety of your life has led you to this moment: the moment that you choose to finally become the person you have always known deep down that you were meant to be. The moment that you release with loving gratitude your attachment to the version of yourself that has gotten you this far; even though that version of you is someone to be proud of, they are not your final destination. There is so much that you have wanted to accomplish, and I know that the life that you have dreamed of is just within your grasp. *This is the moment when you reach out and take it.*

The journey of becoming who you were always meant to be has begun. Now it is up to you to rewrite the story of your life, immersing yourself in shadow work and emerging from the unconscious mind like a phoenix rising from the ashes. For the first time in your life, the next part of your story is entirely up to you.

Endnotes

INTRODUCTION

Page 2. American Psychological Association, "Stress Effects on the Body," November 1, 2018, https:// www.apa.org/topics/stress/body.

CHAPTER 2

Page 17. Christine Comaford, "Got Inner Peace? 5 Ways to Get It NOW," *Forbes*, April 4, 2012, https://www .forbes.com/sites/christinecomaford/2012/04 /04/got-inner-peace-5-ways-to-get-it-now /?sh=2b7bbcec6672.

CHAPTER 5

Page 62. American Psychological Association, "Stress a Major Health Problem in the U.S., Warns APA,"

2007, https://www.apa.org/news/press/releases
/2007/10/stress.

CHAPTER 8

Page 141. Mohd Razali Salleh, "Life Event, Stress and Illness," *Malaysian Journal of Medical Science* 15, no.
4 (2008): 9–18.

Page 141. Linda O'Neill, Tina Fraser, Andrew Kitchen-
ham, and Verna McDonald, "Hidden Burdens:
A Review of Intergenerational, Historical and
Complex Trauma, Implications for Indigenous
Families," *Journal of Child & Adolescent Trauma* 11
(2018): 173–86.

Page 141. Jordan T. Bell and Tim D. Spector, "A Twin
Approach to Unraveling Epigenetics," *Trends in
Genetics* 27 (2011): 116–25.

CHAPTER 9

Page 150. P. Stapleton, J. Dispenza, S. McGill, D. Sabot,
M. Peach, and D. Raynor, "Large Effects of Brief
Meditation Intervention on EEG Spectra in Med-
itation Novices," *IBRO Reports* 9 (2020): 290–301.

Acknowledgments

First and foremost, this book could never have been possible without my husband, Andrew. He is the reason that *Shadow Work* is here, because a feat like this would not have come into being without the unconditional support of my partner and his willingness and ability to take on the work of two parents while I sat down every day to write.

To my children, Juliana and AJ, who graciously allowed their mother to follow her dreams, I am forever thankful.

A huge thank-you to my parents for encouraging me to share the truth about my life and our family; this book would not have been possible without your faith in me. Thank you for being my first teachers and for supporting me in this process.

Thank you to my remarkable agent, Sarah Phair, for being my rock during the process of bringing this book to life. To my publicists, Katerina Zalalas and Kate Marlys, for helping me navigate this process every step of the way, my sincerest gratitude. And my editor, Kate Zimmermann, for approaching me about being the person to write this book, one of the most humbling moments of my life. I cannot thank you enough for giving me this opportunity.

Shadow Work is the culmination of years of attempting to understand how to get to the root source of trauma and heal from the inside out, not just for myself, but for all the people I have been so lucky to do shadow work with. My Shadow Seekers, this book is my sincerest thank-you for trusting me with your care. Being such a small part of your story has been the honor of a lifetime.

About the Author

Danielle Massi, MS, LMFT, is a master shadow work practitioner, motivational speaker, and CEO of The Wellness Collective, a holistic healing space in Philadelphia. Her signature shadow work program, the Create Your Light Academy, continues to help thousands of spiritual women unearth, remove, and heal unconscious blocks that are causing a disconnect between their mind, body, and energy.

Danielle is the founder of the SELF(ISH)philly Conference, a self-care event where hundreds of women gather annually to indulge in a day of expansion and growth, and the creator of the Shadow Seekers® Certification course, which teaches spiritual leaders to become trauma-informed, certified shadow workers.

Danielle has written for and been featured in *New York Magazine's* The Cut, *Shape Magazine,* the Huffington Post, and Buzzfeed, and is a frequent guest on major news outlets and podcasts.

Find Danielle online at iamdaniellemassi.com and on social media at @iamdaniellemassi.